THOUGHT NEVER DIES

For Clemencia

Not for the proud man apart
From the raging moon I write
On these spindrift pages
Nor for the towering dead
With their nightingales and psalms
But for the lovers, their arms
Round the griefs of the ages,
Who pay no praise or wages
Nor heed my craft or art.

ALSO BY JAVED AMIR

The Mask
Writing Across Boundaries
Modern Soap

Thought Never Dies

Hasti ke Mat Fareb Maen Aajaio Asad
Alam Tamaam Halqa e Daam e Khyal Hai

Ghalib do not be deceived by existence
Existence is but a loop in the web of thought

Javed Amir

Published by
Imprint*publishing*
Islamabad, Pakistan

Thought Never Dies

ISBN: 978-969-552-011-6

Published by Imprintpublishing, Islamabad.

Price in Pakistan: Rs. 2200.00
Elsewhere: USD 30.00

Printed in Pakistan

Contents

BOOK REVIEWS

SOME REVIEWS OF AUTHORS' BOOKS

ACKNOWLEDGEMENTS

Foreword

Javed Amir's selection of essays and reviews encapsulate his search for a worldview. His finding is that if the truth being pursued is narrow it flouts wisdom and breeds intolerance of truths found by others. Equipped with the widest possible reading experience, he contemplates the idea of the sacred in the first essay and tells us that it lies in the non-judgmental sphere of life, away from the certitudes that disfigure our souls.

I first saw him in Government College Lahore, a good-looking youth immersed in literature, writing short stories in the college magazine. He stood first in Masters in English in the province, then took the civil services exam and landed in the Foreign Service and trained in Lahore's prestigious Civil Services Academy. I was there too but he was far ahead in the order of merit.

Subsequently, Javed changed his life. He left the Foreign Service at an early age and settled in America. After a struggle that did not dehumanize him he succeeded where most others would have failed. His mind was flexible enough to flit between literature and the stock exchange with ease, accompanied by his wise and understanding wife Clemencia and his wonderfully talented children. When I visited him in Washington, he was living in a capacious house that served as his private domain populated with great literary and political classics.

What has he achieved? Apart from writing his books, more importantly, he has arrived at a wisdom he can live with. Can I say it in a sentence? I will quote from his Introduction: "The beauty of existence is in its constant change and in its erotic energy. Lucretius' immortal poem, which is obviously a tribute to the wisdom of the Greek philosopher Epicurus, clearly begs us to balance a life devoted to the wisdom of thought with the wisdom of the senses."

The second essay talks of mythology, probably secretly aware of the blanket disapproval the Muslims who think they believe only because they have rejected the mysteries of the human soul. He quotes Jung who said, "Religion is a defense against the experience of god. By providing a preconceived notion of god you are denied a larger and deeper experience." Mythology, on the other hand, writes Javed, does not short circuit the transcendent. Mythology is like poetry and therefore flexible. Religion, on the other hand, is inflexible and rigid, the very antithesis of mythology.

In a later Essay, he finds "cosmic religion" in the faith of the Native American, a fine answer to the "hard-shell" Puritanism of the early arrivals in America and a rebuke to his former homeland where the Taliban may soon take over an ideologically vulnerable state. There follow two essays on erotic love backed by the authority of Vatsayana and the semi-divine status of the hetaera accepted jointly by Greeks and classical India.

I read his essay on Toledo especially because I could boast of some knowledge after reading Simon Schama's classic portrait of the city where once the Jews lived in harmony with the Muslims. Javed's sketch from his visit to this "principal city of his mind" is exquisite including the coda regretting how Muslims had become internecine with intolerance in the 21st century. The kind of "education" Javed has put himself through is no longer possible in today's Islamic world where even the states founded as secular societies are relapsing into the medievalism of an "Arab spring".

Like many of us, he is martyr to the magic of García Márquez and sums up in a sentence what I have sought to express after reading the Nobel Prize-winning Colombian novelist: "For someone who has lived both in Pakistan and Colombia, I find striking parallels in the histories of these two countries. There is an uncanny resemblance in the politics and numerous other details of the Gaitan and Liaquat Ali Khan assassinations in that cold war era."

Given the above unfolding, little wonder that Javed should disagree with the worldview embraced by his old country he still loves. He is clear in his mind that Pakistan's set-in-amber foreign policy has become completely unserviceable, and at times argues in vain with Pakistani and Indian diplomats in Washington D.C. obsessed with self-defeating terms like "reciprocity" and "full resolution of disputes."

Javed is passionate about attending book launches and when I was in Washington he took me to his favorite haunt, the Washington D.C. bookstore "Politics and Prose". He writes about the session the bookstore had with Mohsin Hamid, probably the Pakistani writer with the best-crafted prose in English. The short novel "The Reluctant Fundamentalist" went through six drafts. I agree with the comment Javed offered at the launch: "The first question I asked him about his novel was whether he would agree that his characters of Erica and Chris were more allegorical than real persons because they were very thinly drawn sketches. Besides, Changez's capricious love for America mirrored his affair with Erica."

Javed's repertoire is full of books that would be considered anti-American in a conservative United States. I join his enthusiasm for Gore Vidal, arguably the best American essay-writer, and share his enthusiasm for the indictments issued by wise Americans of its rudderless capitalism, its hegemonic "empire" born out of its power-projection abroad. His longest essay is on this subject, apart from the insights Tariq Ali presented during one of his visits to D.C. But there is much else that America teaches that should not be forgotten after the empire declines and disappears, tilting the world into an interim period of directionless chaos and great suffering. Every empire of the past has performed a "civilizing" function, and what America has taught to Javed is the freedom America's founders posited in that most self-consciously intellectual fountainhead called The Federalist Papers.

Khaled Ahmed
Consulting Editor
Newsweek Pakistan
Lahore
13 November 2013.

Introduction

This is a coming of age book—old age that is. As I walk towards the sunset of my life, a faithful Shih Tzu by my side, I am becoming increasingly aware of mortality. Years ago when I was young, I wrote to live; nowadays, do I write so as not to die? I don't think so.

Implicit in the title of this book is the allusion that masterpieces of art, literature and philosophy are everlasting whereas human beings are mortal. In other words, the best of human Thought does not die, but we do. I think that is putting it too simplistically. Let me tell you what I believe as I explore further into this subject from my hermetic abode in the old town of Ellicott City, where most of my essays were conceived and written. I have now spent 35 years around the gilded capital of these United States, covering literary and cultural events as well as writing Book Reviews and Essays. As I look back and read what my book contains, I notice that finally I have become a Washingtonian. Truly belonging to this city has been a long time coming. The Ravi did take a while to flow into the Potomac.

II

Broadly speaking there are three sections in my book. The Essays section maps my spiritual journey, beginning with the attempt at defining The Sacred. With serendipity as my guide, that first Essay led me to discover the Uses of Mythology and A Cosmic Religion. A chance reading of a fascinating book titled, *Gauguin's Skirt* led me to explore Art and the Erotic imagination and then on to a discussion of the boundaries of Sex, Eroticism and Love. Apart from essays on the Many Faces of Global English, a Wine

Drinking Lapsed Muslim, The Magic of New Mexico, there is a piece on a nostalgic trip to Spain's Toledo, a principal city of my mind. Finally, there is literary criticism of the works of my favorite writers like E.L.Menken (who had a summer house in Ellicott City), Gore Vidal (who lived in his grandfather's sprawling mansion in Rock Creek Park), Marcel Proust, Garcia Marquez and Carlos Fuentes (who grew up in DC where his father was a Mexican diplomat).

The Articles section of the book deals with the cultural and literary goings-on in the DC area. It is a glimpse into some of the events that I covered as a journalist at the Smithsonian, the National Gallery of Art, the Library of Congress, Politics and Prose Bookstore, the Brookings Institute, Johns Hopkins University in Baltimore, and the annual National Book Festivals on the Mall. I also have some interviews with visiting South Asian and British authors like the novelist Mohsin Hamid and the political activist Tariq Ali.

Finally, the Section on Book Reviews--which is a careful selection from the 50 or so reviews I wrote for Karachi's *Dawn* newspaper from 2002 to 2010. These book reviews highlight international and domestic political, economic and cultural developments in the first decade of the 21st century from the vantage point of this Town, where elected officials now come not to serve the country but become millionaires. Topics covered are American Plutocracy, Continental Drift, Global Gilded Age, Blowback, Rumsfeld, the Wars in Iraq and Afghanistan after 9/11, Still the White Man's Burden, the 2008 Financial Crisis perpetrated by Wall Street and, in a lighter vein, how the West misunderstood Scheherazade of the Arabian Nights fame.

I have now spent 35 years around the gilded capital of these United States, and finally become a Washingtonian, in part, by writing this book. It has been a long time coming. The Ravi did take a while to flow into the Potomac.

III

The heart of this book, of course, are my Essays which are a foray into the works of some of my favorite writers, artists, painters, philosophers, scholars of mythology and religions, and pantheists. Therein lies the *raison d'etre* of the title of this book. Not only does my book celebrate Art and Thought, but also appreciates the joys and pleasures of a fully lived Epicurean life. Since I do not live a typical American life consumed by time or money, the essential message is that this richly lived adventurous writing life does not come to an end with old age. In fact, it blossoms with old age. As the poet said, Ripeness is All.

Many individuals who live a linear life run only by what the Greeks called 'chromos' or the repetitive ticking of time, devoid of the soaring sublimation of thought and the unplumbed romance of emotions, are merely born at point A, die at point B in time, and then wait, like J. W. Prufrock measuring their life with

Implicit in the title of this book is the simplistic allusion that Thought is everlasting whereas we human beings are mortal.

coffee spoons, to be buried at point C in time. Old age becomes, for these dull souls a period of the living dead, waiting to be buried or incinerated, as the case may be. Not so with me. At least I hope not. Need I remind the reader that I am an avid admirer of Ingres and Renoir who indulged themselves--in their octogenarian years-- painting nudes, invariably of young models.

Therefore, dear reader, I do not lament like Yeats did, when he said

I spit on the face of time that has disfigured me

Or when he wrote this about old age:

O who could have foretold that the heart grows old...
The seed of the fire grows feeble and cold.

Nor do I empathize with even such powerful lines of Dylan Thomas:

Do not go gentle into the good night,
Old age should burn and rave at close of day;
Rage, rage against the dying of the light.

Such an understanding of life does not appeal to me, as aptly put by T.S. Eliot:

Do not let me hear
Of the wisdom of old men, but rather of their folly,
Their fear of fear and frenzy, their fear of possession,
Of belonging to another, or to others, or to God.

Talking of the wisdom of old men, I have a famously admired couplet of a *ghazal* from the great Mirza Ghalib, the 19th century Urdu poet, on the title page of this book:

Hasti Ke Mat Fareb Maen Ajao Asad
Alam Tamam Halqa e Daam e Khayal Hai.
(Ghalib do not be deceived by existence
Existence is but a loop in the web of thought)

This beautiful specimen of medieval poetic thought, to my mind, is tantamount to what Descartes said *I think, therefore I am.* Respectfully, I disagree. No doubt the examined life elevates us from being just animals, but experiencing what the abundant physical gifts of life offer to us humans is important too. To exist in this world you have to be active, to be engaged passionately with our senses. We cannot know ourselves by pure thought alone. Rather, also by what we do. How you live life fully determines your existence, not mere thought. Passion cannot be a slave of thought, as Plato condemned it to be. Besides, Ghalib is being contradictory anyway, and the message of the lines quoted above runs contrary to his own intense appetite and passion for physical pleasures that a lived life has to offer. Describing the moment of near-death did he not say:

Go Hath Mein Jumbish Nahin, Aankhon Mein To Dum Hai
Rahne Do Abhi Sagar-O-Meena Mere Aage
(Though the hands don't move, the eyes are alive
Wine and goblet, let them stay in my sight.)

Secondly, life is not a lie or a deception. It is so only if you have the wrong expectations and beliefs. If you approach life knowing full well that it is far from being perfect, you will have less chances of disappointment and thus enjoy whatever you can. This is what happens to idealists who then end up subsisting on a life of denial and masochism. I believe Gore Vidal put my point of view better than I ever could:

"Because there is no cosmic point to the life that each of us perceives on this distant bit of dust at galaxy's edge, all the reason for us to maintain in proper balance what we have here. Because there is nothing else. No thing. That is it. And quite enough, all in all."

IV

Finally, mortality. Asked about death by a student, Confucius replied, *"While you do not know life, how can you know about death?"* To me the real question is how to live life not to be obsessed with death. I believe that if you have lived life fully, the impermanence of existence ceases to be an unbearable issue. The feeling of loss of our faculties as we grow old is undeniable. However, the fact that we grow old and die, that nothing lasts and time devours all, should actually awaken us to life's infinite beauty.

I am reminded here of an over two thousand year old poem by the Roman poet, Lucretius. *De Rerum Natura* (On the Nature of Things) is a reflection on the fear of death. However, the poem begins with a song to the Goddess of Love, Venus whose arrival in spring regenerates life with an immense erotic desire:

> *The fact that you grow old and die, that nothing lasts and time devours all, should actually awaken us to life's infinite beauty.*

First, goddess, the birds of the air, pierced to the heart with your powerful shafts, signal your entry. Next wild creatures and cattle bound over rich pastures and swim rushing rivers: so surely are they all captivated by your charm and eagerly follow your lead. Then you inject seductive love into the heart of every creature that lives in the seas and mountains and river torrents and bird-haunted thickets, implanting in it the passionate urge to reproduce its kind.

Witness the sense of wonder and passion of this remarkably *modern* poem written thousands of years ago. This wonder did not depend on age-old dreams of an after-life paradise, but of living this earthly life to the full. The realization that all is mortal in our lives, the fact that all is temporary does not render this physical existence insignificant. Or lead us to erroneously conclude that life is a lie or a deception.

Dante's Francesca says about death: *Il modo ancor m'offende* (I shudder at the way of it).

Lucretius, however, says it is foolish to fear death since we will never know we're dead. Death by definition is a state that excludes experience. If you fear death, you fear an illusion. Therefore, love this life and experience the joys of existence, enjoy good food, sex and laughter, relish the conversation of friends, forget ambition and try to live an enlightened life of quiet enjoyment away from the rat race of the madding crowd.

The creative pleasures—and they are so many—some of which like these essays, the residue of wasted time, are the measure of my days. I still write to live. The beauty of existence is in its constant change and in its erotic energy. Lucretius' immortal poem, which is obviously a tribute to the wisdom of the Greek philosopher Epicurus, clearly begs us to balance a life devoted to the wisdom of thought with the wisdom of the senses. At its core, the erotic passion is the affirmation of life even in the face of death and mortality.

The Sacred

Yosemite falls

When I was an artist and a young man, I wrote a short story called *The Dirge of the Stones*. As a twenty year old I had traveled from Lahore with my younger brother to the hill town of Nathiagali in the foothills of the Himalayas. To this day, I have the memory of that evening, when strolling alone in the mountains I had a hierophany as if the hills spoke to me. It was a unique experience something that has lingered in my memory nearly fifty years. In subsequent years, there were similar moments in spectacular locations like *Place du Drummond* overlooking the Mediterranean in South of France or in Patmos and Mykonos, the Greek islands in the Agean sea.

A few years back, however, I experienced an intense communication with nature in the ordinary, small village of Oella next to Ellicott City in Maryland. Having dropped my young son at a book fair at a nearby Mall, I had driven alone to the Old Town up a narrow road winding its way along the Patapsco river. I had a guitar music playing in my car radio, when out of nowhere I was transported into another dimension. As I slowly climbed the Oella Road surrounded by tall oak trees, I could hear the river below first flowing gently and then suddenly with the voice of a hidden waterfall. I stopped the car and crawled down a hundred feet or so through a steep incline and there was the river with prehistoric giant rocks jutting out with the water gushing down into a fall. I sat on a big boulder in the shape of a huge tortoise, transfixed alone.

What was unique was that, of course, I was watching the river and listening to the music it was making, but somehow I also felt that the river and the surrounding little hill packed with tall trees was watching me. Not only was I perceiving but was being perceived. What was this deep spiritual connection with nature? Was this not what is known as the sacred?

Actually, exploring the sacred requires an interdisciplinary approach. You have to don the roles of a poet, a theologian, a geographer as well as a cultural historian. First, it must be recognized that all that is sacred is integrally connected to a place. Any meaningful feeling has to be a placed experience. Second, the enduring identity of a sacred place lies in the stories that have been woven about that place and the power they exert on the mind. Third, merely saying that this is a magical place is not enough. You have to hear the inner voice of the place to make sense of it. In other words, you cannot separate "who you are" from "where you are." I may have affinity to the mountains at Yosemite whereas another person may feel the same in Mecca or Benares. Unless there is this reciprocity between person and place, there are no feelings of the sacred.

> *I may have affinity to the mountains at Yosemite whereas another person may feel the same in Mecca or Benares. Unless there is this reciprocity between person and place, there is no feelings of the sacred.*

As anyone who has experienced the sacred in nature will tell you, this happens accidentally. You cannot deliberately choose a location to have this feeling. I had no idea that I will encounter this blissful feeling as I drove up the hill in Oella village. A simple location (what the Greeks called 'topos') suddenly became an energizing force, drawing an intense connection with your most intimate self (or 'chora'). In a flash you are connected to virtually everything around you. This unexpected connectedness makes you feel that not only you are watching nature but you too are being watched.

This energizing phenomenon is further accentuated when time or 'chromos' which is merely a repetitive ticking of time turns into 'kairos' or an unrepeatable timeless moment which lives only in memory and cannot be experienced again. So much so, that in later life, when you visit the same sacred place you become a tourist to your original intense experience. However, the experience lives on in the memory.

It is thus the remembered place more than the place itself which feeds the mythic imagination about the sacred in nature. How do you share this experience of the sacred with others? You cannot express the ineffable by either being totally subjective or totally objective. It has to be in a language of shared participation, somewhere in between the subjective and the objective. In brief, this experience can only be expressed in the language of poetry what Octavio Paz called "the other voice". "When nature speaks" wrote Heidegger, "it does so with a highly textured and poetic voice." It is in this language of metaphors and symbols that you can express what is essentially a divine-human encounter.

This transcendence can be experienced, among others, in the poetry of John Muir who lived in the Yosemite Valley or Gary Snyder, who wrote about the Pacific Northwest. Most nature poets feel deeply the presence of the place. They all show that their experience was not simply in their minds but was somehow shared in a particular moment by everything around them. John Muir in his poetry speaks "for," "to" and "with" nature:

We are in the mountains / And the mountains are in us.

Talking of mountains, *Tahoma*, the mythic Native American mountain near Seattle or the mythic *Kailash* where it is believed that the Ganges, the Indus and the Brahmaputra originate in the Himalayas, are not locations on any map or chart. These are "mountains within" because the sacred place is essentially non-geographical. They are what Jung called "the mountains of the undiscovered self" or what Thoreau experienced at "Walden Pond," a mountain he only climbed in his dreams

> *It is thus the remembered place more than the place itself which feeds the mythic imagination about the sacred in nature.*

It must be noted, in passing, that for some people this experience of the sacred remains dense and opaque. They cannot see through the masks. Just as they cannot see through the metaphors of poetry or religion. God, after all, is only a metaphor. Another such mask of the sacred is nature. Why do people fail to see the extraordinary in the ordinary? First, this quest requires intense love and a merciless obsession to pursue the hidden reality. Secondly, the ordinary anesthetizes the mind with dull predictability, turning what we see all the time into what we don't actually see. Finally, in our quest for the sacred we have to remember that our destination is not really a place but rather a new way at looking at that place. As T.S. Eliot wrote:

We shall not cease from exploration
And the end of all our exploring
Will be to arrive where we started
And know the place for the first time. (Little Gidding)

To conclude: the essence of a sacred place is its ordinariness. It is something we fail to "see" because it is always seen. Once you pierce through the mask you can experience the different dimensions of place and time. Of course, to see the same place in a hundred different ways is much harder and much more rewarding than visiting a hundred different places and never really "seeing" any of them.

the essence of a sacred place is its ordinariness. It is something we fail to "see" because it is always seen.

The Uses of Mythology

Prometheus is bound and tortured for giving fire to humanity at its creation.

Are you a man of faith?
No, I don't need faith, I have experience.

Simply speaking, myths mean stories about gods. They are the song of the imagination. They are parables, not objective facts. Are they, therefore, factually lies? No, they are not events that happened once in time. Though history and mythology have existed side by side, they are not the same. More to the point myths are events that happen all the time. Imagination is what creates myths just as it creates religion or poetry. To see life as a poem and yourself participating in a poem is what a myth does for you. It is crucial to remember that mythology is not a search for the meaning of life but for the experience of being alive.

What is the source of myths? Just as a dream is a private myth, a myth is a public dream. You could even say that a myth is a world's dream. Both dreams and myths come from the same place: the unconscious. When we dream we are fishing in a vast ocean of mythology. Wrote Blake: "O! how I dreamt things impossible."

Myths create a counter- narrative, a parallel universe, a world of gods so to speak, alongside our daily life. There was a time when there was no ontological separation between the world of gods and quotidian existence. The divine, or what we call today the sacred, was just an aspect of the mundane. The storm with lightening in the sky, the moving waters of a river, human passions like love, rage or sex momentarily lifted humans into a different plane of existence. Humans then saw the world with new eyes.

Was it ignorance or fear that made humans create this parallel universe? When they saw lightening and destruction they called it a god or goddess of fire or even the devil at work like the mythological Hindu Goddess Kali. No, it was not ignorance but more like creating a coping mechanism, an imaginative make believe so that they could deal with the unknown and therefore make life bearable and come to terms with mortality. In this sense mythology was an early form of psychology. No wonder when Freud and Jung tried to psychoanalyze modern minds and feelings they automatically turned to classical mythology and gave it new interpretations to fit our contemporary world.

> *It is crucial to remember that mythology is not a search for the meaning of life but for the experience of being alive.*

There is no one universal mythology in the world. Every culture, every age has its own. Sometimes, older mythologies re-appear in later ones. A comparative study of these mythologies clarifies each of them. For example the virgin birth mystery is much older than Christianity. Buddha is said to have been born from his mother's side. It is obviously a symbolic not a factual birth and signifies a spiritual rather than clinical birth. Why was Jesus known to have been born on December 25? That is the date of the winter solstice, when the nights begin to shorten and the days grow longer. This is the moment of the rebirth of light. Actually, this interpretation is clarified once we come to know that the Persian God of Light, Mithra, was also born on that date.

Is mythology another form of religion? No, mythology is neither theology nor is it about the supernatural. What mythology is all about can be summed up into two words: human experience. Organized religions only address social and ethical questions, not mystical experience. To fill this gap in traditional Islam, for example, we have Sufi Islam where mysticism is the dominant theme. No wonder Jung wrote: "Religion is a defense against the experience of god." By providing a preconceived notion of god, he said, you are denied a larger and deeper experience. Mythology, on the other hand, does not short circuit the transcendent. As we said before mythology is like poetry and therefore flexible. Religion, on the other hand, is inflexible and rigid, the very antithesis of mythology.

Another thing. Religions are not mythologies either. In fact most of them, especially the three monotheistic religions of Judaism, Christianity and Islam have an ambivalent attitude towards being called mythologies. On the one hand, some of their parables are pure myths, on the other hand, they insist that their creed and their prophets are factually based and that they are historical facts. Hinduism is different and accepts mythology and regards history as ephemeral. Buddhism's fables are closest to the tenets of mythology as an early form of psychology whereas Confucianism regarded ritual more important than mythological narratives. Perhaps, the major similarity between religion and mythology, in general, is that both need ritual to provide the right setting for comprehension. Without the transforming rituals both religion and mythology would amount to reading the lyrics of an opera without the music.

II

We live today in a demythologized world where we have lost the true understanding of myth. We fail to realize that mythologies often sprang from profound anxieties of human beings to painful practical problems and that mythologies provided spiritual healing. It was around 500 BCE in the Axial age—a term coined by Karl Jasper-- which fuelled an age of Reason or *logos*, a way of thinking different from *mythos*. Whereas mythology never questioned itself, logos tried to establish the truth through rational intelligence. To Plato, myths were old wives tales; to him only rational discourse brought about true understanding of life. Thus began the rift between *logos* and *mythos,* between reason and faith, between mythology and science a contradiction in western thought that persists to the present day.

> *We live today in a demythologized world where we have lost the true understanding of myth. T.S. Eliot's epic poem,* **The Wasteland,** *aptly captures this demythologized modern world.*

In the modern era, it was in the 18th century Europe that we saw the beginning of the death of mythology. The age of enlightenment denigrated myths as useless, false and outmoded way of thinking. The new heroes of the modern world were scientists and inventors rather than mystics or shamans. Newton's empirical ethos regarded mythology as a primitive mode of thought whereas Marx at a later time saw mythology as a disease of the mind. About this time, without myths and ritual the sense of the sacred also died. Now not only did Nietzsche declare that God was dead but human beings started to live in an infinite nothingness.

> *Garcia Marquez in his splendid work* **Cien Años de Soledad** *challenges the hegemony of* **logos** *over* **mythos** *with his iconic dreamworld of* **Mocondo** *and magic realism.*

T.S. Eliot's epic poem, *The Wasteland*, aptly captures this demythologized modern world. This is a world of 'stony rubbish' where human beings know 'only a heap of broken images.' Today writers and artists, not religious leaders, attempt to re-acquaint us with the mythological wisdom of the past. In reaction to the heartless cruelty of modern day technologically advanced war, Pablo Picasso came up with his historic painting *Guernica* which depicts a secular crucifixion in the 20th century. Today mythmakers like Joyce and Borges uncover the masks of god and see beyond the visible material world. Garcia Marquez in his splendid work *Cien Años de Soledad* challenges the hegemony of *logos* over *mythos* with his iconic dreamworld of *Mocondo* and magic realism. Actually, among others, it was Goethe in *Faust* and Luke Skywalker in *Star Wars* who made it clear that our modern scientific tools, our machines and our computers are not enough. We have to rely on something else also for survival.

In the above-mentioned works, to name only a few, mythology has become an art form –whether it is literature or paintings or even movies--which can transform our lives provided these works of art are understood seriously. These artists have a clear realization that modern day neuroses cannot be cured by logical arguments. Instead they need spiritual healing which mythology can provide. Conrad's masterpiece "The Heart of Darkness" starkly portrayed this lesson when he highlighted the triviality, nihilism and despair of the modern man in Kurtz's dying words "The Horror! The Horror."

Cervantes wrote in *Don Quixote* "dreams are the only reality." Similarly, the hunter-gatherers of the Paleolithic age some 20,000 years ago regarded 'dreamtime' as the only reality. It was their way of re-living the mythical lost paradise, common to many cultures, ancient and modern. For these so-called primitive cultures, prayer and dreamtime were synonymous and experience of these transcendental moments was its own reward. With the hunters, the animals inspired mythology; with the planters of the Paleolithic age, it was plants and above all seeds. This was a revolutionary transformation not only of myths but of human psyche. When you killed an animal, he was dead. End of story. But when a plant was cut, another one sprouted. Here dying led to new life. Thus man came to believe that life and death were inter-twined, that death was not the end of the story. Therefore mythologies sprang up teaching us not to fear death but to enjoy life and its experiences.

Just as the Agrarian mythologies replaced the sky God of the Hunters, the invention of the City resulted in new mythologies. It was around 4000 BCE that Marduk created Babylon and the city became a symbol of the lost paradise. The ziggurat replaced the mountain of the Agrarian age as the center of the sacred. Every city was a holy city. "The Epic of Gilgamesh" told the adventurous tale of Gilgamesh, the fifth king of Uruk, and Enkidu, his servant. Unlike the earlier myths, Gilgamesh reflects upon his own experiences without divine help. With this declaration of his independence from the divine, Gilgamesh carves his own destiny.

> *Just as the Agrarian mythologies replaced the sky God of the Hunters, the invention of the City resulted in new mythologies. It was around 4000 BCE that Marduk created Babylon and the city became a symbol of the lost paradise.*

III

Even today the myths of the past live in us. Some of these stories tell us how ancient people made their rites of passage. For example the ritual of circumcision symbolizes the rite of passage of a boy to a man. When Athena tells Telemachus in Homer's *Odyssey* to go and seek his father, what she is really saying is to de-link from the mother and become his own man. Similarly when Jesus goes to the cross, he is on his way to his father, leaving the mother behind. As a young man growing up in the modern world, the best guidance is provided by writers like Joyce and Mann, who use mythological themes to tackle questions and concerns and problems of the young. Their message is to listen to your heart, not to others or to conventional wisdom. Personally, I can be proud of my decisions in life when as a young diplomat I left a 'secure' foreign-service career and took a plunge into the unknown to follow my bliss. Instead of a bureaucratic life, I chose a life of a literary writer and an explorer of ideas. I make this point merely to suggest that what we are discussing here is not some idealized world of abstractions but the realities of life. Needless to say, even today mythology has relevance in our lives.

> *Most powerful myths are about extremes in life. They force us to experience the unknown, the spiritual and the transcendental. "Unless it is encountered as part of the process of regeneration, of death and birth," writes Karen Armstrong "mythology makes no sense."*

It must be noted that myths contemporary role is not merely ideological or therapeutic. Actually myths are clues to our deepest spiritual potential, able to lead us to delight, illumination and even rapture. Myths teach us to overcome the compulsions of the unconscious, the negative powers of the abyss. You have to be adventurous. What matters is the journey not just the destination. Don't be obsessed with security and material gain. Cross boundaries. Adventure's experience is its own reward. There is an important idea in Nietzsche of *amor fati* or love of your fate. Myths teach that acceptance solves suffering. Forget blaming others for your fate. Forget Freud when he blames parents for your ills. Forget Marx when he blames society for your misfortunes. From Karma mythology to Gilgamesh, mythology proclaims that you have no one to blame but yourself. Not only that, mythologies also teach us how to move on, how to deal with painful rites of passage, from one state of mind to another, from one stage of life to another.

Most powerful myths are about extremes in life. They force us to experience the unknown, the spiritual and the transcendental. "Unless it is encountered as part of the process of regeneration, of death and birth," writes Karen Armstrong "mythology makes no sense." When we quit thinking primarily of ourselves and our own self-preservation, we undergo a truly historic transformation of our consciousness. Mythology repeatedly teaches us to follow our own bliss, our own calling. Don't let others--whether they be parents or society or a bureaucracy-- run your life. Don't be a slave of fools. If you follow an imposed system, you are bound to turn into a dehumanized machine like Darth Vader or a Dick Chaney. You have to be like Luke Skywalker who rejects the imposed system and makes his own destiny.

"Artists" says Joyce "see radiance in all things." Your epiphanies are in Joyce's words "aesthetic arrests". You don't want to possess the object of admiration because that would be pornography says Joyce. You just want to behold it in wonder. Understood thus, myths exist beyond words and images. They are like metaphors. What can be known but not fully told:

The Search

The past
Is but the cinders of the present;
The future
The smoke
That escaped
Into the cloud bound sky.

Be gentle, be kind my beloved
For words become memories,
And memories tools
In the hands of jesters.

When wise men become silent,
It is because they have read
The palms of Christ
In the face of the Buddha.

So look not for wisdom
And guidance in their speech, my beloved.
Let the same fire
Which chastened their tongues
Into silence,
Teach us—teach us.

Myths teach us to overcome the compulsions of the unconscious, the negative powers of the abyss. You have to be adventurous. What matters is the journey not just the destination. Don't be obsessed with security and material gain. Cross boundaries. Adventure's experience is its own reward.

The Magic of New Mexico

Black Mesa Landscape, Georgia O'Keeffe, 1930.

When I first visited New Mexico's central valley, stretching along the Rio Grande from Albuquerque to Santa Fe to Taos I fell in love with the slow, sunlit peace of this savage, Indian land. But it was not before I visited the ancient Taos pueblo— located between the Jimenez and Sangre de Cristo mountains-- with its unique smell of pinyon smoke, that I began to experience the magic spell of New Mexico.

For me the magic of the land was also a flashback to my childhood memories of the village of Harappa in the Punjab where I spent many a summer vacation in the 1950's at my grandfather's 19th century *Haveli*. Like Proust I rediscovered my Combray in the small town of Messila when I looked at the ceiling of a bookshop in the main plaza. The sight of the crooked *balas* reconnected to me to my inner-most and deeper self as if in a dream. The ceiling was exactly like my grandfather's home, the one I had stared before I went to sleep in the dim lantern-lit light as a six year old.

When I visited Abiqui with Clemencia, I knew that this was my country too, as much as it was of the iconic, mythic painter Georgia O'Keeffe. Abiqui was land she indelibly made her own. "As soon as I saw it" she wrote in the 1930's "I knew it was my country. I had never seen anything like that. There is something in the air that is different. The sky is different. The stars are different. The wind is different." For more than forty years she spent every summer and fall in the adobe house in a place called Ghost Ranch. In 1949 she settled permanently in that house, facing the spectacular beauty of the mountain called "The Padernal". She wrote, "God told me that if I painted it enough, he will give it to me."

Another painter by the name of Manyard Dixon sums up the essence of New Mexico in a painting from Taos known as "Old Patio". This painting was done in 1931 from Dixon's New Mexico period which surprisingly lasted only seven months. If you examine "Old Patio" you see a little adobe house with a dirt floor surrounded by the Taos pueblo. The painting seems to say that is all you need in this desert land, a place of shelter, a blanket of warmth, clean water from the well for drinking and chilies drying on the corner of the roof. That is the kind of simple memories one carries away from New Mexico.

The ceiling was exactly like my grandfather's home in the Punjab, the one I had stared before I went to sleep in the dim lantern-lit light as a six year old.

To capture the varied art scene of New Mexico one needs to spend an afternoon walking along Canyon Road which is only a bloc or two away from Santa Fe's main Plaza. The stunning adobe architecture that is ubiquitous here, seems to have been forced by the land itself. Mostly these houses are brown or tan color on the overlay of plaster or stucco with pastel shades of pink and blue. Doors and window trim are often painted blue or turquoise. The interior of the houses is usually painted white. I was amazed by the variety within the adobe form: no two houses looked alike. Since the primitive bloc of mud and straw are too expensive these days, true adobe houses are rarely made. So most modern adobe houses are now built with cinder blocs and two by fours. And yet to the poet's eye, they still look breathtakingly primitive.

The oldest adobe houses were built by Spanish settlers in the 1750's. And that is what is unique about Santa Fe. It was established by the Spaniards moving South to North, rather than by Anglos moving East to West. Today Canyon street is populated by an abundance of art galleries representing hundreds of artists and ranks as one of the most famous art districts in the USA. It is here that the famous *Los Cinco Pintores* which included Will Shuster, Fremont Ellis, among others, who came to live in Santa Fe in 1919. Together in the span of 20 years they gave the town a reputation as a great colony of artists.

It was about the same time, in fact it was 1920, that Mabel Dodge of New York and her native American husband Luhan renovated and expanded a small adobe house in Taos which came to be known as the "Luhan House." Thus began in Taos a famous era in the history of American counterculture. In this house Mabel Dodge supported and entertained artists and writers like Emma Goldman, Alfred Stiglitz and his wife, the landscape-maddened Georgia O'Keefe, the famous photographer Ansel Adams, the world renowned British writer D.H. Lawrence, among others. When I visited the Luhan House and its small library with old furniture from the 1920's it was a deeply poignant experience. The brick courtyard, the tall cottonwood trees with Chinese magpies flying around and the ghosts of all those great artists made it look like a house of spirits. I felt a new part of my soul wake up.

From the Luhan house I walked on the Paseo del Pueblo Norte to the awe-inspiring Taos Pueblo which I knew from Ansel Adams' famous black and white photographs. The Taos pueblo has been home to the Tewa-speaking Taos Indians since about 1100 A.D. and has been one of the oldest continuously inhabited communities in America. I had never experienced Native American history and life as I did that day. In the middle of that village, where stood a cottonwood grove, a little sparkling stream was flowing. I was reminded of Francis Livingston's stunning painting "San Geronimo Day" which captures the Pueblo in all its intimate grandeur. At the Pueblo, as luck would have it, I was treated to the Camache deer dance which began in a thrilling way with costumed men each leaning forward on two short sticks, thus simulating a four legged creature.

> *The oldest adobe houses were built by Spanish settlers in the 1750's. And that is what is unique about Santa Fe. It was established by the Spaniards moving South to North, rather than by Anglos moving East to West.*

No visit to Northern New Mexico -- or what is known as El Norte-- is complete unless one drives on the "High Road" between Taos and Santa Fe. It is on this road that you experience 19th century colonial New Mexico with its old adobe farmhouses with pitched metal roofs and to your left are stunning views of the Sangre de Cristo mountains. Ancient villages dot this spectacular road. There is the Picuris Pueblo where the Anasazi settled about 750 years ago. There is the town of Truchas, clinging to the side of the Canyon with magnificient views of the 13,000 foot Truchas peaks. You can even see in the distance-- if you look to the north -- the grey green mesa cutting the Rio Grande Gorge, a sheer-walled Canyon that drops 800 feet to the Rio Grande. And, finally there is the village of Chimayo where lo and behold the Catholic faith is practiced outdoors by a stream, next to El Santuario (The Shrine) where a miracle about Virgin Mary had occurred in 1814.

I knew the miracle and the magic was in the land itself. And to make the land glow, there is the golden light which attracts photographers and painters from all over. Here in New Mexico you never see a mountain right beside you. It is always too near or too far. In the early hours of the morning, before the sun is up over the Sangre de Cristo mountains in the east, I can see miles of sunlight already on the western land mass.

Santa Fe and Taos are not only art colonies where literary tradition is revered but what is more significant is that the life of the mind is not a suspect here as, for example, in other parts of the USA. People are really friendly and open-minded and interested in you, and yet they leave you alone. It is this unique world-view that enables visual arts, performing arts and literary arts to flourish at the same time.

In her Taos house, Mabel Dodge supported and entertained artists and writers like Emma Goldman, Alfred Stiglitz and his wife, the landscape-maddened Georgia O'Keeffe, the famous photographer Ansel Adams, the world renowned British writer D.H. Lawrence, among others.

On Canyon Road in Santa Fe there are 250 galleries for a local population of only 80,000. Here one meets painters, writers, sculptors and photographers all living in adobe houses which some locals jokingly call "mud-hut nuts." These are people to admire. They live a life of slow talk and easy rhythm what is called "poco a poco" lifestyle. New Mexico, in fact, is not a land of one culture but an intersection of three. Here Spanish Americans, Anglo Americans and Native Americans live in a splendid tri-cultural harmony. What is unique about these writers and artists is that they have created in the American public a respect for the Indian culture and an awareness of the past.

"New Mexico" wrote D.H. Lawrence, "changed me forever…Curious as it may sound, it was New Mexico that liberated me from the present era of civilization, the great era of material and mechanical development…The moment I saw the brilliant proud morning shine high up on the deserts of Santa Fe something stood still in my soul, and I started to attend." It has been said that if Shakespeare had ever seen the night of the stars in Santa Fe, he would have gone mad trying to improve upon his "Look, how the floor of heaven is thick inlaid with patines of bright gold…"

Esssay 4

A Cosmic Religion

Voice of the Sipopu, William Schuster, 1934.

In his writings titled "The Soul of an Indian," Ohiyes, the renowned Native American poet of the Spirit says: "Our religion is the last thing about us that the white person will ever understand." Undoubtedly, he was reacting to the first missionaries that came in contact with Amerindian spirituality and branded it as "pagan" and "devil-worshipping." Not surprisingly, therefore, first the Spanish church and later the Anglicans demanded that Native Americans renounce their gods as false and accept the Christian faith.

What was shocking to these white invaders, wrote Ohiyes, was that the Indians had no priests, no dogma, no proselytizing, no persecutions, nor were there any scoffers or atheists among them. Above all, there were no temples or shrines. Instead all worshipping took place in the open. Indeed these "savages" deemed it a sacrilege to build a house for what they called "The Great Spirit." In their religion, according to the Native American poet, the Indians believed that their gods could be met face to face in the mysterious aisles of the primeval forest or in the sunlit bosom of the virgin prairies, on the dizzy spires of the naked rocks and in the vast jeweled vault of the night sky. Such a God, he wrote, needed no lesser temple.

In the American Southwest, there are twenty one Pueblo Indian nations as shown in a map from a beautifully illustrated book "The Storyteller" by Mary Packard. Most prominent of these are Hopi, Zuni, Taos, Zia, Acoma, Laguna and so on. This little book contains stories from the Anasazi which are essentially a grandfather or a grandmother narrating bedtime stories to children. However, as you read through the lines you discern a more sophisticated and profound mythology. In these stories you discern a quest for a meaning of life, the appreciation of beauty, the power of solitude, the reverence for silence, the lack of greed for material possessions, the sympathy and spiritual communion with the animal world, the preservation of nature, the absence of fear or terror of death and, above all, the profound love for the earth. As a Hopi saying goes: *The One who tells the stories rules the world.*

> *Most of us are trained to read with our rational minds. But there is another way to read, where words take on a life of their own and the sound becomes the meaning as in listening to music.*

One of the striking differences in these stories is the experience of the Indian oral tradition as compared to western written languages. Most of us are trained to read with our rational minds. But there is another way to read, where words take on a life of their own and the sound becomes the meaning. This is a way of reading that is akin to listening to music, where the sheer power of the sound can move the listener to tears. This difference between oral and written means of perception is at the heart of the difference between the magical and the mechanical world-view. Whereas the oral is spontaneous, the written invariably appears labored or rational like a treatise that can be analyzed and understood later on. Since the nature of sound is inherently ephemeral, the process of maintaining reality has to be highly participatory. In other words, it is almost like the South Asian style of recitation of poetry.

John Cahill of the University of Alberta narrates an incident where he was constrained to preserve in writing a rare, overpowering ritual practiced by some Indian tribes in Canada. His attempt failed miserably since he could not capture in writing the effervescence of the passing oral word. The experience of this oral tradition is unique and lasts only as it is rendered. Once the experience is over, it is hard to recreate it in writing. No wonder the western scientific and analytical mind cannot figure out the spirituality of the Native American.

One major theme of this spirituality is the quest for Creation's center or the sacred center. The ancient myths, for example, of the Navajo tell stories of four or more worlds which existed long ago below the level of present life on earth. Thousands of years ago, certain figures began an upward journey and came to live on this earth. The place where they emerged continues to serve as a vertical *axis mundi*. For the Navajo, among others, this sacred center exists somewhere near the four corners, where the states of Utah, Colorado, New Mexico and Arizona meet. I have seen a hand-drawn map that shows this place of Emergence as a mythical or imaginary mountain at the intersection of the co-ordinates of four actual mountains. This sacred center is the center of the earth and can only be seen by the eyes of the spirit. It does not exist as a geographical fact, yet paradoxically, it is a place more real than real.

Another important theme of Amerindian spirituality is its adoration of silence unlike our western life's endless conversation and chatter. Of course, silence can definitely be terrifying if you are in a prison or in solitary confinement. But there is another gentler type of silence that is more like silent reflection. This silence of choice is a reverent communion or form of meditation not with an absence but a deeper form of presence. The modern man, of course, shuns this kind of silence which he

> *This sacred center is the center of the earth and can only be seen by the eyes of the spirit. It does not exist as a geographical fact, yet paradoxically, it is a place more real than real.*

would find boring and even exasperating. In fact, I am myself guilty of putting music on the radio or what have you, as soon as I find myself alone in the house. Even as I walk in the woods with my dog, I plug my I-Pod into my ears. According to Hoopa Indians, at night your soul wanders in silence seeking a gentle heart so that when morning arrives the soul is reluctant to return to the body. An Indian was never ready for the day to start until he meditated in silence with a humming song.

Yet another aspect of the Amerindian religion is its compelling attachment to land. When asked by a white man, "Who owns this land?" Chief Ohiyes replied, "We do not own the land; the land owns us." William Carlos Williams struggled all his life to understand this mystique of the Indian religion but words failed him to comprehend it:

"The land" he wrote, "don't you feel it? Doesn't it make you want to go out and lift dead Indians tenderly from their graves, to steal from them…. some authenticity."

Modern man's materialism denies him Native American's consciousness. This worldliness has made us lose not only our souls but also a fuller humanity. Love of the earth and a sense of wonder at nature could teach us what Walt Whitman wrote:

"To her children the words of the eloquent dumb great mother never fail."

One such modern man who heard this authentic spiritual voice of the *eloquent dumb mother* was D.H. Lawrence: "In this oldest religion—one that predates Greeks, Hindus and even Egyptians—everything was alive not supernaturally but naturally alive....There is no God, no conception of a god... all is god."

In 1922 when he first saw the desert and mountain landscape of Santa Fe and Taos in New Mexico, Lawrence was in a state of rapture. "It is curious" he wrote, "that it should be in America –of all places—that a European should really experience a permanent feeling of religion." After all, the first and foremost root meaning of religion is an experience to come into naked contact with the very life of air, which is the life of the clouds and so of rain. This Cosmic religion of man's pre-war days precedes the god concept and is therefore greater and deeper than we know.

the heavens were as calm as a lonely heath
the waves of the sea rolled on, as if to breathe
the sultry atmosphere
presently the horizon was enveloped in darkness
it spread on the yawning foam of the ocean
the pleasant breeze shook the silent atmosphere
it began to rain
O Great Spirit such blissful scenes are
but an adoration of your loveliness
the starry sky, the silent night
the howling wind, the fearful storm
how the world lives and moves
makes us believe that there is something
greater than we know.

This is a sonnet, *Storm by the Sea,* I wrote in 1962, at the age of 17, and was my first poem published in Lahore (Pakistan).

> *When asked by a white man, "Who owns this land?" Chief Ohiyes replied, "We do not own the land; the land owns us."*

Art and the Erotic Imagination

"The Dream" by Picasso.

Very few novels begin so erotically: *Lolita, light of my life, fire of my loins. My sin, my soul. Lo-lee-ta: the tip of the tongue taking a trip of three steps down the palette to tap, at three, on the teeth. Lo. Lee. Ta.*

In this novel, Nabakov makes us see that by sheer routine sex we wear out the beauty and magic of a world whose very existence ought to have been a perpetual unending mystery and surprise.

Speaking of surprises, I have always been obsessed by the mysteries of the body and the mind, the power of the aesthetic and erotic imagination. In this essay I wish to explore briefly how the erotic imagination has shaped art and culture of the human race. What follows are few snatches of literature, music, opera, theater, cinema, poetry, cultures of East and West and, above all some famous paintings highlighting the themes, symbols, passions and objects of the erotic. As one can imagine, the subject is so vast that to do it justice one would have to write a book.

In Woody Allen's movie "Husbands and Wives", the female protagonist says: "If you say you lusted after me then why did you not fall in love with me? Can the two feelings really be separate?" Is erotic love then a form of lust? Luxuria, the latin word for lust is one of the seven deadly sins. It was the bible that talked of the sins of the flesh like adultery, masturbation and homosexuality. Hieronymus Bosch's extraordinary painting "Triptych of the Garden of Earthly Delights" (Prado, 1500), exposes the problematic boundary between erotic love and lust. In the vast luminous landscape of this painting there are dozens of naked humans and the sin of lust is exemplified by a couple making love in a huge transparent bubble. The theme of the glass sphere can be associated with the famous Flemish proverb "Happiness is like glass and soon breaks."

Is erotic love then a form of lust? Luxuria, the latin word for lust is one of the seven deadly sins.

Contrast this painting with the work of Gauguin in the late 19th century. As I discussed in my detailed essay on Gauguin elsewhere in this book, he evoked in his paintings and sculptures a kind of sexual paradise in which nakedness or sex has nothing to do with lust or sin but is as natural and effortless as picking a flower. This allure of the erotic can also be seen in the paintings of Delacroix, Ingres and Gerome. In 1857 Charles Baudelaire dedicated his collection of poems, *Les Fleurs du Mal*, to his gay friend and master, Théophile Gautier. Following a trial for obscenity, *The Flowers of Evil* rightly became the most famous book of erotic poetry published in nineteenth-century France. The French Enlightenment had always encouraged erotic writing, of the kind found in Voltaire, Diderot, and Laclos (*Les Liaisons Dangereuses*). It was looked on as an elegant proof of sophisticated manners and civilized values. Sex, was regarded no more than a form of witty conversation.

II

The subject of the young girl at her bath combining the themes of nudity, innocence, purity and libido is one of the great erotic visions from the Greek Sirens to Botticelli's "Birth of Venus" to Anita Ekberg wading in the Trevi fountain in Fellini's 1960 classic "La Dolce Vita." The theme of the *beauty in the bath*, in all its variations, provides an excellent pretext for having a good sensual look at those parts of the male or female body normally hidden from view by clothing. Among paintings, Ingres' "Turkish Bath" (1863, Louvre) which he painted when he was 82 years old is a culmination of the powerful vein of eroticism in the entire work of this extraordinary painter. The oriental setting of the dozens of nude women offers a range of sensual pleasures: music, dance and swimming naked in the water of the pool.

Youthful eroticism is considered rather reductively, I think, as the best period of one's life. The other day as I sat with some friends at a roadside café, admiring the young girls pass by, I was taunted for being a filthy old man. We used to look at girls, I was reminded, when we were young. In art, however, loving couples of any age live in an atmosphere of erotic enchantment, tenderness and happiness. There is no age limit for experiencing pure joy. This reminds me of Chagall's painting "Lovers in the Park" which I believe is in a private collection in St Petersburg in Russia. In this self-portrait the artist is *embracing his beloved*, Bella, when he was advanced in years. What is striking about the painting is that it portrays an embrace of total sincerity and immersion into his beloved so that Chagall is completely invisible and lost in the portrait and all you see is his shadow and the prominent face of Bella only. In the painting the colors grow on you. They get warmer and warmer with passion and emotion. The simplicity and harmony of the intense colors make this a unique painting and can be regarded as one of the most poetic homage to love.

The memorable dance scene between the old and death-obsessed Prince of Salina (Burt Lancaster) and the young and vivacious Angelica (Claudia Cardinale) in Luchiano Visconti's all time classic movie *The Leopard* conveys to perfection the vortex of eroticism, passion and sensuality. That dance is similar to Renoir's famous painting "The Ball at the Moulin de la Galette." The freshness of the brushstrokes conveys a joyous animation, while the physical contact between the dancing couples shifts the emphasis towards an increasing eroticism. Carrying even further this theme of *dance and the erotic*, let me mention Matisse's "The Dance" at the Hermitage, which depicts five nude women in a lyrical and serene dance. The circle of dance of these girls, faceless and timeless, involves us in a simple circular rhythm that seems endless.

> *In art, however, loving couples of any age live in an atmosphere of erotic enchantment, tenderness and happiness. There is no age limit for experiencing pure joy.*

The post-impressionist painter Henri de Tolouse-Lautrec lived out his life in the *brothels of Montmarte* in Paris and produced a prodigious number of paintings of the low life of the *café chantans* between 1889 and 1899. "At the Moulin Rouge" (1892) is perhaps his masterpiece. The colors are so luxurious and erotic that there is a lyrical release into fantasy and the figures drift into an enchanted world as if in a dream. On the other hand, Picasso's depiction of the brothel situated on Rue d'Avignon in Paris in his grotesque "Demoiselles d'Avignon" is ugly and almost anti-erotic.

The fact is that from the Greek hetaira to the Venetian *courtesan* to today's call girl, the sex worker has rarely been depicted with humanity or dignity. Saadat Hassan Manto's deeply humanistic short stories about the red light district inhabitants of Lahore was definitely an exception. Like Lautrec, Manto depicted these women without any moral judgment. I can also think of Mirza Rusva's famous 19th century Indian novel "Umrao Jan Ada" where the protagonist is a cultured Lucknow lady and like a Japanese geisha or Veronica France of 17th century Venice an accomplished poet along with being a professional courtesan.

> *The fact is that from the Greek hetaira to the Venetian* **courtesan** *to today's call girl, the sex worker has rarely been depicted with humanity or dignity.*

Talking of Lautrec I was reminded of a recent Pakistani painter, Iqbal Hussain who was born and brought up in *Heera Mandi*, the Montmarte of Lahore. Since the 1970's Hussain has painted prostitutes but there is no eroticism in his work. These are realistic, dispassionate portraits without any joy of sex, rather of the victims of the sins of sexual trade. These outcast women are shown mostly in broad daylight, fully dressed, trying to make ends meet in husbandless, fatherless households. They are neither beautiful nor happy nor does the artist arouse any sentimental sympathy for them. However, he does try to humanize them and give them respectability. In his iconic work "The Birth of a Prostitute" (Lahore Art Gallery, 1995) all you have is a devastating irony. A trumpet looking like a phallic symbol is being played in celebration of the birth of a female wage earner.

Worlds apart, on the other hand, Mozart's masterpiece "The Abduction from the Seraglio" which is a comic opera sung in German takes place in a harem. The West's fascination with indolent, fleshly women in languid sensual surroundings was a favorite theme of art via the Ottoman Empire in the 18th and 19th centuries. Ingres' "La Grande Odalisque" (Louvre. 1814) is a profane work of art where the long back of the nude woman in a oriental setting evokes mysterious *erotic pleasures of the harem.*

Before I conclude this section of my essay, a word about *autoeroticism* or the so-called regressive form of eroticism. To some, the voyeur or the exhibitionist is a pathological perversion of the erotic. Historically, masturbation has been treated with negative connotations following the Biblical condemnation of "Onanism" where Onan was punished by God with a death sentence for "scattering his seeds on the ground" to avoid having children. However, in this day and age it is difficult to castigate exquisite artists like Caravaggio, Dali or Picasso when they portray the autoerotic in some great works of imaginative art. Dali's surrealistic painting "The Great Masturbator" (Madrid, 1929) is loaded with erotic symbols and reprises a part of Bosch's "Garden of Earthly Delights." And then there is Picasso's "The Dream" (1932, New York Ganz Collection) with its rich warm colors showing a blond woman giving herself solitary pleasure by manual stimulation. Like Dali, needless to say, Picasso was also interested in taboo erotic subjects.

As a genre, erotic art is still evolving. Historically, great art—from the novel to poetry to photography to the cinema -- has been mistakenly excoriated as obscene and *pornographic*. However, movies like Bertolucci's "The Last Tango in Paris" or Fellini's "La Dolce Vita" can hardly be termed as porn nor can we call Joyce's "Ulysses" or D.H. Lawrence's "Lady Chatterley's Lover" smut. It is important to distinguish between porn intended as

> *Essentially Kama Sutra is a book on the philosophy and aesthetics of love. In keeping with Hindu philosophy, the art is openly erotic.*

an aphrodisiac and a more figurative, subtler, more intellectual eroticism that relates to interpretation rather than crude exhibition. For a long time, Modigliani's nudes were vulgarly considered as pornographic. His "Red Nude" (1917, Venice) is less about overt nudity—although there is an immense sensuality in this work—and more about the mood reminding one of Tuscan art of the Renaissance.

III

"Sex" says Vatsyayana " is the most wondrous gift of God and men and women must learn to make it such" (Kama Sutra, 4th-5th century AD). At the superficial level this Hindu sex manual can easily be misunderstood as pornographic. But properly understood there is nothing prurient here. Essentially Kama Sutra is a book on the philosophy and aesthetics of love. In keeping with Hindu philosophy, the art is openly erotic. Kalidasa's famous poem "The Birth of Kumara" has an entire canto of 91 verses titled "The Description of Uma's Pleasure" which describes in graphic detail the lovemaking of the divine. The Pallava and Chola bronze sculptures unabashedly celebrate the divine beauty of the human body.

Islam, however, had a different view of sexuality. It divided the mind from the body, and the sensual from the metaphysical. Like early Christianity, Islam focused on the sinfulness of the flesh and the dangers of sexuality. Yet, when Islam came to India it did not suppress the Hindu tradition of erotic writing. In 18th century Delhi the Mughal emperor Muhammad Shah II had painters make miniatures of himself in the act of having sex with his mistress. Later on, in the same court, the courtesan Ad Begum appeared completely naked at parties. As Dalrymple has pointed out, it was not during the Islamic period that the dramatic break with India's erotic tradition occurred. Instead that change took place during the British colonial period in India with the arrival of the evangelical Christian missionaries in the mid-19th century.

> *In our modern materialistic times, money has corrupted eroticism. It has become a department of advertising and a branch of business. Capitalism has turned Eros into an employee of Mamon.*

It was the Christian monastic view of Chastity that invariably represented woman as a diabolical temptation for lust and sin. For the devout monk, love of God replaces the siren call of the senses. However, just as in Sufi Islam, poets like Waris Shah sublimate physical love into mystical ecstasy, the intertwining of divine and human love is beautifully expressed in a famous passage of her life by Saint Teresa of Avila. Here she recounts the appearance of an angel:

In his hand I saw a long golden lance, and at the end of its iron tip I seemed to see a tongue of fire. He appeared to run this through my heart several times, so that it penetrated to my entrails. When he extracted the lance, I felt …engulfed in the flame of God's great love. The pain was so intense that I moaned several times. It is not a physical pain, but a spiritual one, even though the body has a part in it.

Those of us who may have seen the Canadian movie "Agnes of God" would truly appreciate the repressed unconscious undertones of this passage.

IV

In our modern materialistic times, money has corrupted eroticism. It has become a department of advertising and a branch of business. Capitalism has turned Eros into an employee of Mamon. Today erotic love is threatened with dissolution not by the church or so-called morality, but by promiscuity, which turns love into a pastime and a cheap, banal entertainment. Money has turned love into slavery and the balance between the body and soul, between life and death has been rift apart.

The dualism of Eros and Thanatos is one of the great themes of erotic art. The terminal illness that befalls Mimi in Puccini's opera *La Boheme* is the perfect affliction for playing out this theme of love and death. Poetry, theater and painting have provided us with many images of tragic lovers, for whom the culmination of passion is reached precisely at the moment of death. During the English Enlightenment, the tragedies of Shakespeare were often chosen by painters for their work. One such painting by Joseph Wright "Romeo and Juliet, the Tomb Scene" (U.K. 1790) depicts the final scene of the tragic lovers inside a crypt capturing the intense emotional tension with chiaroscuro light clearly borrowed from Caravaggio. As Romeo lay dying, Juliet manages to extract a last kiss, and then hearing voices approach, kills herself with a dagger: "Noise again! Then I will be brief."

Here the experience of the erotic in art is neither an escape from death nor a denial of the terrifying aspects of eroticism. Actually it is an attempt to integrate body and soul into a whole. This wisdom of the senses is what D.H. Lawrence left us as his legacy in a remarkable poem that he wrote shortly before his death. "Bavarian Gentians" is a poem that celebrates a mythical girl who each spring returns from the underground palace of Pluto and Persephone to the surface of the earth, the place of her origin, where death and life embrace:

Reach me a gentian, give me a torch!
Let me guide myself with the blue, forked torch of this flower
Down the darker stairs, where blue is darkened on blueness
Even where Persephone goes, just now, from the frosted September
To the sightless realm where darkness is awake upon the dark
And Persephone herself is but a voice
Or a darkness invisible enfolded in the deeper dark
Of the arms Plutonic, and pierced with the passion of dense gloom,
Among the splendour of torches of darkness, shedding
Darkness on the lost bride of her groom.

(Readers who want to hear this poem read masterfully may like to go to: http://www.youtube.com/watch?v=gbT5UoEy8wA or just Google: Bavarian Gentians by D.H.Lawrence)

Sex, Eroticism and Love

Seated Woman by Egon Schiele

Years ago in a trip to Prague, I saw a painting on display in the Nardoni Gallery. It was the work of a little known early 20th century painter from Austria, Egon Schiele and was titled "Seated Woman with Left Leg Pulled up." I was struck not only by the stark nakedness on display, but by the unabashed gaze of piercing sensuality of the woman. It was a desperate expression of the erotic, an intense desire to grab hold of life, as if the painter knew his life would be short. As it turned out, Eagon Schiele did die very young.

As I discussed in the preceding essay there is a strong link between eroticism and death. In this essay, however, I want to explore the boundaries of sex, eroticism and love? Needless to say, there is an intimate connection between the three. For instance, there is no *human* sexual love without eroticism. On the other hand, animal sex need not have any erotic component to it. Only sex with eroticism makes it human.

One can better understand the erotic by comparing it to poetry and language. If poetry is eroticism of language, eroticism is poetry of sex. Sex, as we know, is solely for procreation, whereas eroticism has nothing to do with procreation; it is primarily for pleasure. The sole purpose of language, on the other hand, is to communicate. But when you transform language into poetry through human imagination its sole purpose of communication is transformed into a form of communion. Poetry's ultimate aim is not to communicate but to be. Poetry exists as art for art sake. When it communicates it does so at a different level, it communicates not as news or as information of facts or as an exchange of ideas but as a form of fusion. It is a participatory discipline.

Just as sex and eroticism are not the same, love is different from both eroticism and sex. You can love your country, for instance, without any sex or eroticism involved. But that is an abstract concept and not human to human love. In the 12th century European courtly love tradition—of which Dante's poetry is an example—love is shown as pure and refined without any carnal pleasure or involvement of the body. But that kind of ascetic or purely aesthetic love –which was profoundly influenced by Muslim Spain with its Sufism and love of a beloved as a path to union with God—became obsolete. Shakespeare's contemporary, John Donne no longer put the beloved on a pedestal but in a bed to experience love in its totality. As he put it: *not to dream all the dream; let's act the rest.*

Today, as we discuss Sex, Eroticism and Love we know that the oldest of these three, the most basic, is of course, primordial sex. Love and eroticism are derivatives of the sexual instinct. However, both of them transform sex into something else more wholesome and mysterious. Both love and the erotic originate in the senses, but do not end with the senses. As John Donne said about the senses:

"Though they are ours; they are not wee."

Understood thus, the erotic act separates from the sex act. It is sex but something more. Obviously as we said before, that "more" is called pleasure. But its essential metaphor is ambiguous. There is mystery in the erotic. It points to many things but always there are two underlying themes: one, of course, is pleasure, the other is death. That is what Egon Schiele's painting in Prague hit me with. It defined the erotic as an attempt to escape from the fear of death.

There is mystery in the erotic. It points to many things but always there are two underlying themes: one, of course, is pleasure, the other is death.

II

The human mind has an infinite capacity to enjoy the *five senses* which are intricately connected through the deepest strata of the brain to the erotic. There is the erotico-auditory bliss in the allurement of the human voice which sounds especially sonorous in the dark when our hearing is enhanced because our sight is impaired; there is this incredible connection between the nose or olfaction and sex through the chemical known as pheromones or sexual odors which excite; the eye yearns to grasp, to undress to caress and in the extreme the so-called "evil eye" can become an ocular vampire; finally, taste and touch are also integrally related to sexual experience. No wonder in Joseph Conrad's novel "Lord Jim" there is this revelation by one of the practical minded characters: "Only a woman can satisfy all the five senses at the same time."

> *Where love is a choice; eroticism is acceptance. Love goes beyond mere acceptance of a desired body and seeks the soul in the body and the body in the soul. In other words, whereas the erotic seeks only the body, love seeks the whole person.*

Here is a brief extract from Joyce's *Ulysses* to give us some understanding of *taste* and *touch* and how they intricately relate to human sexual and erotic experience:

O wonder! Coolsoft with ointments her hand touched me, caressed: her eyes upon me did not turn away. Ravished over her I lay, full lips full open, kissed her mouth. Yum. Softly she gave me in my mouth the seedcake warm and chewed. Joy: I ate it: joy...Screened under ferns she laughed warmfolded. Wildly I lay on her, kissed her: eyes, her lips, her stretched neck beating, women's breasts full in her blouse of nun's veiling, fat nipples upright...She kissed me. I was kissed. All yielding she tossed my hair. Kissed. She kissed me.

Me.

In short, the erotic is a complex multi-sensual experience and a metaphor for human existence. Let me quote Nobel Laureate Octavio Paz on this subject: "Eroticism" he says, "is a rhythm, it separates itself from sex as well as returns to sex, a return to the place of origin where life and death embrace. Bodies like powerful rivers or like peaceful mountains, images of a nature at last satisfied, caught at the moment of harmony with the world and the self that follows sexual climax. Solar happiness: the world smiles. For how long? The time of a sigh: an eternity. The erotic beyond is here and it is this very moment. All women and all men have lived such moments; it is our share of paradise."

Dare I say that this ecstasy is realized through the wisdom of the senses, which—as we know from my last essay-- D.H. Lawrence sought all his life:

> *There is a paradox in that love is a mixture of a mortal body and an immortal soul. This is love's subversive nature. By commingling the material and the spiritual, love subverts both heaven and earth.*

And she felt him like a flame of desire, yet tender, and she felt herself melting in the flame. She let herself go. She felt his penis risen against her with a silent amazing force. She yielded with a quiver that was like death, she went all open to him. She quivered again at the potent inexorable entry inside her. So strange and terrible. It might come with the thrust of a sword in her softly opened body, and that would be death. She clung in a sudden anguish of terror. But it came with a strange slow thrust of peace, the dark thrust of peace and a ponderous, primordial tenderness, such as made the world in the beginning. And her terror subsided in her breast, she held nothing. She dared to let go everything, all herself and be gone in the flood.

III

How then do we differentiate between the erotic and love? Marcel Proust's classic novel A *La recherche du Temps Perdu (The Search for Lost Time)* is about the love of Swann and Odette. Swann suffers from a delirium. He is madly in love with Odette because she is inaccessible, not her body but her soul. Odette is always the distant other. Swann's love remains incomplete and unrequited because love requires the whole person. In Joyce's novel, *Ulysses*, Molly, is all woman, the perpetual wellspring, the mother earth, and excuse me for saying this, the great cunt who is both Penelope and Venus. She is the borderline that separates love and eroticism. As we know, love is an attraction to a unique person and an attraction both to a body and a soul of that person. Where love is a choice; eroticism is acceptance.

Love goes beyond mere acceptance of a desired body and seeks the soul in the body and the body in the soul. In other words, whereas the erotic seeks only the body, love seeks the whole person. And that exclusivity, that choice of one unique person is the hallmark of love which separates it from the erotic.

Molly's torrent of words is a great affirmation of life and the erotic but not of love as can be seen from this last utterance in the novel:

O and the sea the sea crimson sometimes like fire and the glorious sunsets and the figtrees in the Alameda gardens yes and all the queer little streets and pink and blue and yellow houses and the rosegardens and the jessamine and geraniums and cactuses and Gibraltar as a girl where I was a Flower of the mountains yes when I put the rose in my hair like the Andalusian girls used or shall I wear a red yes and how he kissed me under the Moorish wall and I thought well as well him as another and then I asked him with my eyes to ask again yes and then he asked me would I yes to say yes my mountain flower and first I put my arms around him yes and drew him down to me so he could feel my breasts all perfume yes and his heart was going like mad and yes I said yes I will Yes.

> *In a fire the flame is the subtlest part. It moves upward like a pyramid.*
>
> *Whereas sex lights the fire and raises the flame of eroticism, if you look closely*
>
> *This in turn feeds another flame, trembling and blue: the flame of love.*

Needless to say, when you are in love, there is no 'as well him as another.'

What makes us fall in love to that one person is the age-old question. Plato, following Ibn Hazim of Cordoba, author of *The Necklace of the Dove*, would say that we fall in love at the sight of physical beauty. Love desires beauty. This desire is a search for the possession of the best. Or, perhaps there is a secret chemistry involved in this attraction ranging from the warmth of the skin to the taste of his or her lips. Ultimately love is not a mere carnal or Platonic desire for beauty but a yearning for completion. Both man and woman look to reunite with their lost half. In the final analysis, it is hard to explain the origin of love. According to Dante, love is an accident. The same thought is echoed by Ghalib when he says:

Ishq per zoar nahin / Hai ye wo aatish Ghalib /
Jo lagai na lagai / Aur bhujai na banai.

Needless to say, why we love one particular person and not the other ultimately remains a mystery.

Finally, there are still more mysterious characteristics of love. There is a paradox in that love is a mixture of a mortal body and an immortal soul. This is love's subversive nature. By commingling the material and the spiritual, love subverts both heaven and earth. Then there is the question of choice and predestination in love. If love is an accident, how can we talk of choice? Is there not a continuous struggle in love between fate and choice, between freedom and servitude, between body and soul. In love everything is dialectic, everything is a duality, and yet love strives to be one. One incredible result of this dialectic is how love transcends the erotic. Since the erotic is based on the physical body it is –as we saw in Eogon's painting- terrified by death. It cannot handle the interplay of Eros and Thanatos. Love on the other hand is both physical and spiritual. It can and does look death in the face. As Dylan Thomas wrote:

Though lovers be lost; love shall not
And death shall have no dominion.

Dare we say, love conquers death?

Earlier, I stated that poetry is a form of communion, not communication. When a poem ends it produces silence. In love, the contradiction between communication and communion is even more striking. Yes, love is different from the erotic, but human love is not possible without the erotic. It is through the erotic that when we have sex that our bodies become infinite and we lose our identity. Actually this is a circular experience: it begins with the abolition of the bodies of the lovers and then a moment later, we are back to our bodies. In other words, erotic love is a trance-like experience. As John Donne put it in his classic poem "Extasie":

Love's mysteries in soules do grow
But yet the body is his booke.

In short we humans need both body and soul, both love and erotic sex. Sex is the original, primordial fire. In a fire the flame is the subtlest part. It moves upward like a pyramid. Whereas sex lights the fire and raises the flame of eroticism, if you look closely this in turn feeds another flame, trembling and blue: the flame of love.

Toledo: A Principal City of my Mind

Storm Over Toledo by El Greco

The last time I visited Spain, I had promised myself to come back and explore Toledo for a longer time. That passionately beautiful island-fortress had stayed in my memory as some principal city of my mind. So last winter, as the bleak winds of war gathered their frenzied pitch in snowy Washington, I escaped to the half-deserted medieval magic of Toledo.

One of the best ways to enjoy this unique city is to wander in its streets, dipping into the treasures of art around you. Toledo is like a huge tapestry that depicts all the elements that have contributed to the development of the Spanish civilization. Built on a granite hill surrounded on three sides by a gorge of the Tagus River, its history is recorded in stone.

The whole city is a network of cobbled streets which have changed little since El Greco painted his famous "View of Toledo" in 1575. The city is surrounded by partly Moorish, partly Gothic walls and gates. Many buildings in Toledo are of Moorish origin like the Alcantara Gate and Bridge or the Alcazar, the rebuilt fortress-palace which still retains traces of its Islamic past.

The painter El Greco worked here and his 16th century house and garden are well preserved. Part of Cervantes' novel Don Quixote is set in the local landscape of La Mancha. But more of that a little later. Under the Moors and later under the kings of Castile, who made it their chief residence, Toledo was a centre of the Moorish, Spanish, and Jewish cultures which co-existed peacefully for centuries. Its School of Translators was world-renowned where scholars from around the world gathered to translate into Latin the long lost works of Aristotle, Euclid and Ptolemy. Needless to say, it was from Moorish Toledo that much of the learning of Hellenic times was transmitted to Europe although most modern-day Spaniards don't like to hear that.

Only recently the Spanish have begun to approach their Islamic past. Actually they take pride in their 'sangre pura' or pure blood. No Spaniard wants to face the thought of Moors in the family tree. However, they are finding that much of what they think of 'pure Spanish', their architecture, their temperament, their poetry, music and even their language is a blend from a long Arabic heritage.

In 712 AD Tariq took Toledo, then the greatest city in Spain, from the Catholic Visigoths without a fight. Almost all of Spain by then was called al-Andalus. (This was the Arabic name for Islamic Spain, not to be confused with the province of Andalucia.) For 400 years Toledo remained a stronghold of the Moors and Spain enjoyed a degree of cultural excellence unsurpassed in the rest of mediaeval Europe. Music, literature, philosophy, mathematics and medicine flourished. The work on Arabic medicine, mathematics and metaphysics was to draw a primitive Europe out of the decadence and ignorance of the Middle Ages.

For centuries later, the works of Ibn Sina (Avicenna), Ibn Rushd (Averroes) and Ibn al-Arabi influenced thought in the west, even if Dante had to lodge them in his purgatory. Ibn Sina (980-1037AD) was a Neoplatonist whose *Canon of Ibn Sina* remained Europe's standard medical textbook for 500 years. Ibn Rushd (1126-1198AD) was a follower of Aristotle whose commentaries on the Greek philosophers were to influence European thinkers like St Thomas Aquinas. Ibn al-Arabi (1165-1240AD) was a mystic who taught that all life is one being which is the divine and that therefore all religions are one and the same:

My heart is capable of every form:
A cloister for the monk, a fane for idols,
A pasture for gazelles, the votary's k'aba,
The tables of the Torah, the Koran.
Love is the faith I hold, wherever turn
His camels, still the one true faith is mine.

Today Spanish linguists acknowledge that although Ladino, the tongue of Sephardic Jews, and Colo, that of the gypsies who came later to Spain, are gone or debased but many Arabic words live on. Words such as 'guitar' are derived from the Spanish 'guitarra' which is derived from the Arabic 'qitar.' The famous Christian Knight El Cid is derived from 'al-Sayyid' or lord. The familiar cry Ole! Ole! at the bullfights does descend from Allah! Allah!

Then there is the popular hybrid Mudejar architecture in Spain. This Mudejar style of architecture is a lavish blend of Arab and Gothic architecture. Its high salons, arches and alcoves were worked in yeso, an art that Arabs mastered, carving plaster walls with breathtaking patterns of flowers, geometrics and calligraphy. In Toledo a classical example of this Mudejar style is the 12th century Puerta del Sol (Sun Gate) with typical blind arcades and two contrasting horseshoe portals. Finally, Arabic poetry in its lyric forms, zajal and muwashshah, is said to have inspired the first ballads of the European troubadours. The deep songs of the Gypsy flamenco, still echo in Spain the moods and rhythms of this lost heritage.

I stopped musing about the Moors in Spain and I took a cab that drove me along the highway on the opposite side of the Tagus, crossing over the St Martin Bridge. The view of the city standing like an island-fortress encircled by the river Tagus is one of the spectacular sights in Spain and one immortalized by El Greco is his landscape "Storm Over Toledo".

El Greco actually came here from Greece and was enchanted by the city and stayed and painted some of the great classics of visual art. He died here in 1641. Today his work and his fame is synonymous with his adopted city. On the outskirts of Toledo is the town of *Alcala la Vieja* which in 1547 was the birthplace of Cervantes. It was with Miguel de Cervantes that the modern literary era was born.

> *For centuries later, the works of Ibn Sina (Avicenna), Ibn Rushd (Averroes) and Ibn al-Arabi influenced thought in the west, even if Dante had to lodge them in his purgatory.*

His creation, *Don Quixote*, is practically unthinkable as a living being. And yet, as Milan Kundera has observed, "in our memory, what character is more alive?" Widely regarded as the birth of the modern novel, *Don Quixote* chronicles the famous picaresque adventures of the errant knight and sane madman, *Don Quixote de La Mancha* and his faithful squire and wise fool, Sancho Panza, as they travel through 16th century Spain.

The cab was now rolling across the red earth of *La Mancha*. I started to listen to a tape of *Don Quixote* read by the internationally acclaimed actor, Edward De Souza. In the distance, I could see country homes, known as *cigarrales*, surrounded by broad cultivated fields and fruit orchards.

However, the tape reading transported me to another time and another world and I realized why *Don Quixote* had haunted readers' imaginations for nearly four hundred years.

Truly the debt owed to Cervantes by literature is immense. I think Cervantes stands for everything that is gentle, forlorn, pure, unselfish, and gallant. His parody of mankind's delusions has become a paragon. As V.S. Pritchett has observed: "Don Quixote begins as a province, turns into Spain, and ends as a universe. The true spell of Cervantes is that he is a natural magician in pure story-telling."

> *May be it is too much to ask the Muslim world to embrace the inclusive spirit of Cordoba, Granada and Toledo of 9th century Muslim Spain to overcome the sectarian cancer that is today devouring its children.*

After the cab ride, I retreated into the cold, gray streets of Toledo. I was reminded of what is called in the west as the "Re-Conquest" and what Ferdinand of Aragon and Isabella of Castile did to the liberal and peaceful civilization of coexistence of the Moors. These two Catholic rulers viewed Muslims and Jews as threats. Under their rule, they established the Spanish Inquisition. For three centuries thousands of Muslims and Jews were killed. An estimated three million people were driven into exile. In due course Spain fell a victim to its own cruelty. History's lesson, often forgotten, is that even great powers are mortal. On arriving back in Madrid, I heard that the Bush administration had launched its War on Iraq. (April 2003).

Update: July 2013.

Since I wrote this essay a decade ago, several books have come out on the spirit of pluralism of Islamic Spain most notably Maria Rosa Menocal's book "The Ornament of the World: How Muslims, Jews and Christians Created a Culture of Tolerance in Medieval Spain."

Given the current Middle East politics, where everything is a fight to death, whether it is in Egypt, Syria, Libya or Iraq, there seems no middle ground. May be it is too much to ask the Muslim world to embrace the inclusive spirit of Cordoba, Granada and Toledo of 9th century Muslim Spain to overcome the sectarian cancer that is today devouring its children. Recently the Beirut daily an-Nahar carried an article by the Lebanese journalist, Hisham Melhem who, like my visit to Toledo, recalls an emotional visit to the Great Mosque of Cordoba in southern Spain, wondering what happened to that sublime culture of peaceful co-existence and how the Arab Muslim world had degenerated into such chaos and repression in the 21st century.

Esssay 8

A Wine Drinking lapsed Muslim

A Book of Verses underneath the Bough,
A Jug of Wine, a Loaf of Bread--and Thou
Beside me singing in the Wilderness--
Oh, Wilderness were Paradise enow!

I was born in the USA on Valentine's Day and I am a proud American. My father, a wine drinking, tennis-playing South Asian lapsed Muslim moved to suburban Dullsville with my mother who is a devout, practicing Catholic from Spain. They are so different from the people around these United States that I sometimes wonder what on earth this so-called *liberal* couple is doing here. Their life style and world-view is such an oddity to our strict social values that one questions as to what happened to the dictum. "When in Rome, do as the Romans do." But as they say, everything is possible in America.

When I ask my dad why does he drink wine if he is a Muslim, he gives me a lengthy scholarly answer. He refers to the so-called English version of *Tafsir Ibn Kathir* which, according to him, indicates an ambivalence in Quranic injunctions. He says the verses of the Quran on this subject show that it was permissible to imbibe strong drinks from date palms and grapes before they were forbidden. He proclaims to be a follower of Jalaludin Rumi, a 13th century Muslim Persian Sufi poet who, he asserts glorified drinking in his poetry. And then of course, there was *Ghiyāth al-Dīn Abū al-Fath ʿUmar ibn Ibrāhīm* or Omar Khayyam in short! I don't believe a word he says because I know at heart he and my Mom are just plain gypsy pleasure seekers.

These fun-loving world travelers met, of all places, in *Palais de Gaulois* in Brussels and got married on a trip to exotic Senegal. Little did they care about their humongous religious and racial differences. As you can guess she is white and he is brown. Fortunately, I resemble my mom more than my dad. For God's sake, human beings fought hundreds of years in the Crusades to validate this titanic clash of civilizations. What a shame they have no respect for mankind's glorious past.

> *I agree with pundits on Fox News that President Obama is a Muslim and he is Malcolm X's love child.*

After committing this incongruity, they now want me to study both Islam and Christianity like some other freakish interfaith families in America. I wonder if they understand the implications. I, for one, agree with the Catholic priest in Dullsville Church and the Imam of the nearby Mosque that this will not work. Any hybrid religion like the Mughal emperor Akbar's wacky *Deen-e-Ilahi* (The Universal Religion of God) is doomed. On the contrary, in their phony, avant-garde minds my parents believe that this is the only way to connect me to my plural identity and dual cultures. You tell me what good is all this going to do to a proper American of this day and age especially after 9/11?

I agree with pundits on Fox News that President Obama is a Muslim and he is Malcolm X's love child. There is no doubt about it that radical Islam is subverting America and its economy by taking our jobs. The French government is absolutely right to ban burqas as are the Swiss in prohibiting the building of minarets near the Alps. It makes absolute sense not to allow the construction of an Islamic center near New York City's Ground Zero. What if there are strip clubs next door. It is still hallowed ground and we should disallow another place of worship for the Saracens.

Have we forgotten the lessons of the medieval times when popular poems like Chanson de Roland depicted the Saracen Zaragoza worshipping a trinity of devils named Mahomet, Appolin and Tervegant? Have we forgotten our love for Salman Rushdie's *Satanic Verses* which glorified our western fantasies of the myth of Mahound?

Clearly my parents are trying to cheat history. My dad often quotes some dude called Joyce who said: "History is a nightmare from which I am trying to awake." As you might have guessed by now, they are too liberal for my taste. To begin with, you can't call these guys immigrants. That is too déclassé a word for these so-called international citizens. If you ask me, international bums would be more appropriate. My father's favorite TV ad is: Life is harsh, your wine shouldn't be.

I don't agree with my dad when he tries to rationalize the fact that today nearly half of Americans have an "unfavorable" view of Muslims. According to his "elitist" world-view, Muslims are just another of a long line of persecuted minority groups in America -- from Catholics in the 19th century to the Jews in the early 20th century. He dreams of Moorish Spain and the supreme peace that prevailed for centuries between Muslims, Christians and Jews in cities like Toledo and Seville. One day, he says, his dream will come true in America.

> *Clearly my parents are trying to cheat history. My dad often quotes some dude called Joyce who said: "History is a nightmare from which I am trying to awake."*

What America is going through today is only a spasm of Xenophobia, he says. That is a temporary reaction to hard economic times and not what America is all about. In time, he says we will learn to respect the "other" and reject Islamophobia, Latinophobia, and Homophobia. The current hullabaloo manufactured by the Tea Party is politically motivated and always surfaces at election times. America is re-visiting "McCarthyism". Today the whipping boy is Islam. Then it was Communism.

My father is a funny guy. He is so 1960's. He writes articles about goofy subjects like multiculturalism and diversity as being good for the future of America. According to him, American mainstream is not white but mulatto culture. I disagree with him. The election of a black President is no proof of a multicultural America. It was just an accident. Had Lehman Brothers not gone bankrupt and the economy not collapsed six weeks before the election, McCain and Palin would be in office today.

What my dad fails to comprehend is that this country has two founding pillars: Judeo-Christian religion and the White race. Man, I was born here and I don't care for no illegal aliens. I felt really sorry for Mr. O'Sullivan, our Irish neighbor, the other day. When a Latino couple moved next door, he was all depressed and dejected and remarked: "Soon I will be the only white guy left in Dullsville." I think the federal government should stop aliens from third world countries migrating to the United States and kick out those here illegally like France is expelling Romanie gypsies.

What I resent most is when people call America a secular state. We may be materialistic but secular, no way Jose'. And the funny thing is that when my dad forced me to visit Pakistan, those naïve folks had no clue either. Since we have Hollywood and Playboy magazine, those suckers thought we are all kafirs or atheists. I wish I could drive them in a typical American street on a Sunday to see all the vibrant and beautiful churches that we Americans go to worship.

In Dullsville we live by faith. In our immediate neighborhood there are four churches, much like those Mosques in Lahore. But thank God they don't wake you up in the wee hours of the morning with loudspeakers blaring at you like those Musalmans do. There is the Lutheran Church, the Presbyterian Church, the Korean Church and, of course, St. Anthony's Church.

The parishioners are devoted Christians. They do not fall into liberal traps like family planning. Take the Visconti family. Regular church-goers. Out of the last fourteen years, thirteen saw a new child being added to that devout family. Papa Visconti has witnessed the proud moment when there was a Visconti child in each grade in St. Anthony's school. Alleluia.

I know my dad would joke at this phenomenon of blind faith, but in spite of our differences I do love him. This is not really his homeland. He was not born here. Dullsville is my home. I am the true patriotic American. Anywhere you dig this land you find rocks, pebbles and sand. This is so because Dullsville is located in the bed of an ancient river, of which the nearby creek is the last reminder. On summer days when me and my dad play tennis, the woods behind the court with the creek in the distance is a picture out of heaven.

In Dullsville we live by faith. In our immediate neighborhood there are four churches, much like those Mosques in Lahore.

The Many Faces of Global English

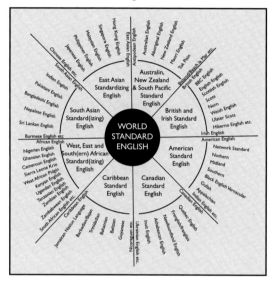

In 1582 Richard Mulcaster, headmaster of Merchant Taylor School in England, wrote, "The English tongue is of small reach, stretching no further than this island of ours." At that time English was spoken by about four million people and stood fifth among European languages with French, German, Italian and Spanish ahead of it.

Today English has emerged as an international political and cultural reality with an estimated two billion people using it as a means of communication, if not as a symbol of their identity. With globalization and widespread use of the Internet, English dominates the world as no language ever has. As late as the 1950s, at the height of the cold war, no one expected this language to acquire such universal stature. Why has it suddenly become the *lingua franca* of the world? Why was it not French, for example, or Mandarin Chinese with its 900 million native speakers for that matter?

Yes, there are more native speakers of Hindi, Chinese or Spanish today but it is English that they have to speak when they go beyond their linguistic boundaries and it is English that they must teach their children to become global citizens. Says Mark Warschauer of UCLA, Irvine: "English has become the second language of everybody. Now to be educated anywhere in the world means to know English."

Secondly, English has become a global language not because of the number of people who speak it. It is much more to do with who those speakers are. Nor is there any inherent intrinsic superiority like a wealth of synonyms or some alluring shades of meanings, as some linguists mistakenly claim, that made it become global.

English has become international for one fundamental reason: the political power of those who speak it as a mother tongue — especially their military power. This has been true throughout history. The reason Greek became the dominant language in the Middle East some 2000 years ago was not due to the intellectual standing of Plato and Aristotle but because of the military conquests of Alexander the Great. Similarly Latin spread throughout Europe because of the Roman military might and Arabic became the language of the Middle East, North Africa and parts of Europe owing to the conquests of Islamic armies.

> *English has become a global language not because of the number of people who speak it. It is much more to do with who those speakers are.*

Although these languages were spread through military might, they were sustained and developed through economic power. Thus British colonialism spread English to the four corners of the globe from the seventeenth to the nineteenth centuries, but it was the emergence of the US as the leading economic power in the twentieth century which established English as a worldwide language. During this time, American media, advertising, motion pictures, popular music, higher education centers and recently the Internet have firmly placed English as the undisputed world language.

Not only does the US contain four times as many native English speakers than any other country, it exercises a greater influence on the way English is developing worldwide than does any other regional variety including the British purist's dream of the imagined excellence of the "Queen's English". This gives discomfort to many native speakers in the UK, Australia and Canada and even to some non-native speakers in South Asia who express worries in their national media about the onslaught of "Americanisms".

First of all, what these critics fail to realize is that there is the closest of links between language and power. If anything were to disestablish the military or economic power of the US, there would be inevitable consequences for the global stature of English. Secondly, as pointed out in his classic study The American Language H.L. Mencken writes that it was "Americanisms" in the early seventeenth century which paved the way for an expanded and mixed vocabulary in English which enabled it to adopt modifications and flexibility leading to its present day global status.

Mencken was contemptuous of what he called the "Anglomaniacs" who failed to understand that language was a living organism. Thus when the American English borrowed words from the native Indian languages in the 1610s like caribou, moose, raccoon, squash, squaw, tomahawk and so on, it was expanding the horizon's of the language and opened it to winds of linguistic change in totally unpredictable ways.

By the late eighteenth century when Noah Webster was compiling his dictionaries there were hundreds of words which were known in the US but not in England. Pronunciation had begun to diverge quite markedly and spellings were in the process of change. Today there are thousands of differences between British and American English — "two cultures" as Dylan Thomas famously remarked, "separated by the barrier of a common language".

What was started by American English or what Mencken deliberately called *The American Languages*, has today proliferated into dozens of world Englishes. The US sociolinguist Braj Kachru suggests three concentric circles representing different ways in which world Englishes have been acquired and are currently used.

> *What was started by American English or what Mencken deliberately called* **The American language** *has today proliferated into dozens of world Englishes.*

The inner circle which consists of native speakers of about 500 million people includes the US, the UK, Canada, Australia, New Zealand and South Africa. The outer circle of about 400 million non-native English speakers in more than 50 countries consists of India, Pakistan, Nigeria, Bangladesh, Singapore, among others. Here English is not a 'foreign language' but a 'second language' since it has a special status in government, in the courts of law, media, business and so on. Writers from South Asia who sometimes call English a foreign language should heed this distinction to avoid confusion.

The third concentric circle which Kachru called the 'Expanding circle' consists of countries like China, Russia, France, Germany, Japan and many more where English is regarded as an international language. These countries have little or no colonial experience with the English language nor does English have any administrative status in their governments. For this expanding circle, therefore, English is a 'foreign language'. The best example of this is "Euro-English" which is now the official language of the European Economic Community.

As users of these three concentric circles of English language surge towards more than a hundred countries and the two billion mark there is also a tremendous contradiction building up. Out of these two billion only 20 per cent use it as a mother tongue. Eighty per cent use it as a foreign or additional language. A number of consequences have, therefore, become apparent.

The first unintended consequence of the Englishes of the diaspora is that they represent a repertoire of cultures and not one monolithic, Eurocentric one. Secondly, it has been argued that English as an international language is being shaped as much by non-native speakers as by native speakers and the variety of Englishes that are emerging will not be rooted in geography and national sense of any native speaking country but is cosmopolitan in nature. It follows, therefore, that the 1986 lament in Ngugiwa Thiong's *Decolonizing the Mind* where he preached that "Africa must stop the west from stealing the treasures of our mind to enrich their languages and cultures" has been overtaken with lightening speed and English now belongs as much to the African as to the British or the American.

> **The first unintended consequence of the Englishes of the diaspora is that they represent a repertoire of cultures and not one monolithic, Eurocentric one.**

Today, the only possible concept of ownership of the English language is a global one and the only possible standard world English will be one that straddles across boundaries. Albert Baugh's *History of English Language* provides hundreds of examples of English words derived from Italian, Spanish, Greek, Persian, Hebrew, Arabic, Hungarian, Hindi, Urdu, Bengali and even Chinese. Such is the capacity of English to absorb new words and modifications that it is hard to find anyone much concerned with foreign words or so-called jarring "Americanisms" now. (See review of my novel *Modern Soap* by my late friend Basit Haqqani elsewhere in this book).

As English spreads around the world will it be able to maintain its present form? Probably not. But why should it? Today the notion that anything is gained by fixing a language is cherished only by pedants or what the Americans call "word nerds." As discussed, among other factors, it is the very anarchy of English that made it the dominant language of the world today.

The varieties of world Englishes has now reached bewildering proportions. From West African English, Caribbean English and South Asian English, to name a few of non-native Englishes, to Australian English, New Zealand English, Canadian English, South African English, and within Britain, Irish, Scots and Welsh English of native speakers — these are all somewhat like dialects except that they are dialects on an international scale spoken and written by millions.

This anarchy for some scholars raises the specter of fragmentation. They argue that eventually English could break up into a range of mutually unintelligible languages as Latin did by giving rise to various Romance languages such as French, Spanish and Italian some one thousand years ago. Although it is impossible to predict the future of English, one thing is certain. With English characterized as it is today by complexity, hybridity and constant change there cannot be a strict linguistic structure or code, as for instance, enforced by the Academie Francaise in France or what is sometimes referred to as "standard English" or "Queen's English" in the English speaking worlds.

It is interesting to note that about 70 million people in South Asia are competent in English today. Within the next generation there will be more speakers of English in this part of the world than there will be in Britain. In this context, Raja Rao was one prescient South Asian novelist who looked forward to the development of what he called a new Indian English. In 1963 he wrote: "English is not really an alien language to us...We cannot write like the English. We should not. We cannot write only as Indians."

> *It is interesting to note that about 70 million people in South Asia are competent in English today. Within the next generation there will be more speakers of English in this part of the world than there will be in Britain.*

Later, Salman Rushdie too wrote that "the children of independent India use English as an Indian language." By subduing the language of the colonizer, as John Updike put it in *The New Yorker,* there has been an explosion of South Asian literature in English during the last 40 years. Like American English earlier, South Asian creative writers today are reinventing a new kind of English, one that is both local and international, indigenous and global.

It is paradoxical that with the mushrooming of world Englishes the need for being bilingual has acquired a new meaning. The fear that the hegemonic power of English would result in the demise of minority languages appears to have been unfounded. Actually a proficient bilingual speaker has a sharper perception of reality because he is bifocal. Given their cultural translatability and a new cosmopolitanism, international varieties of English express national identities and are a way of reducing the conflict between intelligibility and identity.

García Márquez

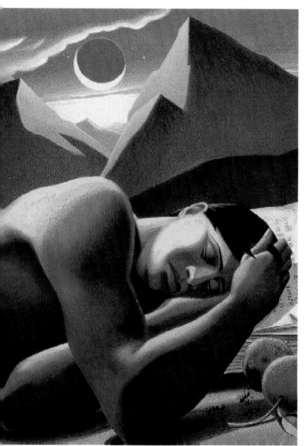

The cover of HarperPerennial's One Hundred Years of Solitude.

"Situated in mystical Latin America, Macondo is a sleepy village where flowers and solitude fall like rain, the decrees of dictators control space and time, and poets hallucinate machines to remember a craftily slipping reality."

It is a commonplace of literary criticism that no writer is equal to his book. In fact according to Faulkner, a writer's life is quite irrelevant to his work. Not so in case of Nobel laureate Gabriel García Márquez whose bestseller memoir "Living to Tell the Tale" (*Vivir para Contarla*) vividly demonstrates that it was precisely his precocious childhood surrounded by a large eccentric family that made him a writer of novels.

For Marquez, like Proust, to write is to remember. Stringing his sentences with words which are more like pearls as beautiful as one can imagine, this masterpiece of a memoir narrates the struggles of the artist as a young man, who against the wishes of his parents wanted to become a writer. As always this book is poetically rendered from Spanish into English by longtime Marquez translator Edith Grossman.

Living to Tell the Tale is part one of a trilogy that Marquez plans to write. It begins in the 1950's but meanders back and forth to his childhood days in the 1930's. As a young journalist from the Caribbean coast of Colombia, he lived a life of dire poverty in Bogota, the distant mountainous political and literary capital of Colombia which was not too friendly to him as a *costeño* (or coastal person). When his first story appeared in the national daily, *El Espectador* he did not even have five centavos to purchase a copy.

The memoir begins with a journey that Marquez undertook with his mother back to the Caribbean village of Aracataca where he was born, to help her sell their ancestral dilapidated house. This Conrad-like heart-of-darkness journey through the swamps of the Magdalena river takes us back to Marquez's magic world of *Macondo*, the mythic town of *One Hundred Years of Solitude*. As we know, that novel won him the Nobel Prize in 1982. It can best be described as an epic poem of an earthly paradise of desolation and nostalgia and seems to have been born during that journey to his ancestral village:

> *"Cien Años de Soledad" can best be described as an epic poem of an earthly paradise of desolation and nostalgia and seems to have been born during that journey to the novelist's ancestral village:*

"The first thing that struck me when we arrived in Aracataca was the silence. The reverberation of the heat was so intense that you seemed to be looking at everything through an undulating glass. My mother remained in her seat for a few more minutes, looking at the dead town laid out along empty streets, and at last she exclaimed in horror: 'My God.'"

All of us have read memoirs sometimes full of boring self-indulgence but Marquez's work is a rare specimen of a writer dealing honestly and intimately with his past. Now 80 years old as he looks back, he is surprised how he survived the loneliness, the whoring and drinking and smoking of 60 cigarettes a day:

"I was convinced my bad luck was congenital and irremediable, above all with women and with money, but I did not care, because I believed I did not need good luck to write well. I did not care about glory or money or old age, because I was sure I was going to die very young, and in the street."

As is self evident, Marquez writes his memoirs with the simplicity, serenity and ease that are the hallmarks of a master. He read Faulkner's *Light in August* and Joyce's *Ulysses*. These novels "provided invaluable technical help to me in freeing language and in handling time and structure in my books."

He writes that Kafka not only cast a spell on him but taught him that *"it was not necessary to demonstrate facts... 'Metamorphosis' in a Borges translation was Scheherazade all over again, not in her millenary world where everything was possible but in another irreparable world where everything had already been lost."*

After he read *The Thousand and One Nights*, Marquez says he learned and never forgot that we should read only those books that force us to re-read them. Turning to his life as a young man he says he had two addictions: smoking and sex. Here is how he narrates, with a chuckle, an adventure with a policeman's wife:

"I remember her first name was Nigromanta... she had an Abyssinian profile and cocoa skin. Her bed was joyful... and she had an instinct for love that seemed to belong more to a turbulent river than to a human being. Her husband had the body of a giant and the voice of a little girl... and he had a bad reputation of killing liberals."

Among other tales of people, journalist colleagues and places, the memoir also narrates in detail a first hand account of the traumatic assassination of the Colombian hero and Presidential candidate Gaitan in Bogota on April 9, 1948. It was a horrific event that started a civil war between the rich and the poor in Colombia which lasts to the present day. Incidentally, on that fateful day both Fidel Castro, a young leftist from Cuba and US Secretary of State, George Marshall, were both present in Bogota. Writes Marquez: "I believe that on April 9, 1948 the 20th century began in Colombia."

> *For someone who has lived both in Pakistan and Colombia, I find striking parallels in the histories of these two countries.*

For someone who has lived both in Pakistan and Colombia, I find striking parallels in the histories of these two countries. There is an uncanny resemblance in the politics and numerous other details of the Gaitan and Liaquat Ali assassinations in that cold war era. The onset of civil war in Colombia in 1948 caused a similar widespread bloodshed just as the Partition unleashed human slaughter in the Indian subcontinent in 1947. What appears fantastical in the novels of Garcia Marquez such as the hallucinatory town of Macondo "where flowers sometimes fell from the sky in place of rain" and "swamps thick with lilies oozed blood when you hacked them with machetes" is in fact a normal description of much of the third world in our times.

Marcel Proust and Lost Time

What we call the beginning is often the end
The end is where we start from...

Writing about childhood, Wordsworth says: "Nothing can bring back the hour/ Of splendour in the grass, of glory in the flower." Proust, on the other hand, felt that we can bring back that magic hour of childhood and youth if we experience what he called *souvenir involontaire* or involuntary/unconscious memory. This he explained was radically different from voluntary memory where we use our brains to recall past events, people or places through logical, rational reconstruction. That manner of recall, says Proust, is at best partial in its success and fails to capture the "essence of the past." It fails the test of communicating to us "the deepest layer of our mental soil."

Here is the iconic passage from Proust's *A La Recherche du Temp Perdu* which used to be translated as *Remembrance of Things Past* till Roger Shattuck gave us a more precise rendering: *In Search of Lost Time*.

Many years had elapsed during which nothing of Combray, save what was comprised in the theatre and the drama of my going to bed there, had any existence for me, when one day in winter, as I came home, my mother, seeing that I was cold, offered me some tea, a thing I did not ordinarily take. I declined at first, and then, for no particular reason, changed my mind. She sent out for one of those short, plump little cakes called 'petites madeleines,' which look as though they had been molded in the fluted scallop of a pilgrim's shell. And soon, mechanically, weary after a dull day with the prospect of a depressing morrow, I raised to my lips a spoonful of the tea in which I had soaked a morsel of the cake. No sooner had the warm liquid, and the crumbs with it, touched my palate than a shudder ran through my whole body, and I stopped, intent upon the extraordinary changes that were taking place. An exquisite pleasure had invaded my senses, but individual, detached, with no suggestion of its origin. And at once the vicissitudes of life had become indifferent to me, its disasters innocuous, its brevity illusory — this new sensation having had on me the effect which love has of filling me with a precious essence; or rather this essence was not in me, it was me. I had ceased now to feel mediocre, accidental, mortal. Whence could it have come to me, this all-powerful joy? I was conscious that it was connected with the taste of tea and cake, but that it infinitely transcended those savors, could not, indeed, be of the same nature as theirs. Whence did it come? What did it signify? How could I seize upon and define it?

> **Not love, not friendship, not worldly achievements but only through art — rather, only through the meditations to be found in art — that Proust finds a regaining of time, of recovering, re-possessing what is otherwise and always lost time.**

This feeling of a waking dream is the best way to describe this unconscious memory which, unexpectedly in a chance encounter with a hidden sound or smell or in the above quotation from taste of a madeleine cookie, bring back all the powerful sensations and feelings that we felt at a previous time. What is the true nature of this experience will always remain a mystery because it exists outside time. Only the unconscious memory allows the narrator, Marcel to discover days that were long past, the time that was forgotten and, therefore, lost.

Witness in the following words the power of how the unconscious memory engulfs the narrator and how like a flood he relives the past:

And once I had recognized the taste of the crumb of madeleine soaked in her decoction of lime-flowers which my aunt used to give me (although I did not yet know and must long postpone the discovery of why this memory made me so happy) immediately the old grey house upon the street, where her room was, rose up like the scenery of a theatre to attach itself to the little pavilion, opening on to the garden, which had been built out behind it for my parents (the isolated panel which until that moment had been all that I could see); and with the house the town, from morning to night and in all weathers, the Square where I was sent before luncheon, the streets along which I used to run errands, the country roads we took when it was fine. And just as the Japanese amuse themselves by filling a porcelain bowl with water and steeping in it little crumbs of paper which until then are without character or form, but, the moment they become wet, stretch themselves and bend, take on color and distinctive shape, become flowers or houses or people, permanent and recognizable, so in that moment all the flowers in our garden and in M. Swann's park, and the water-lilies on the Vivonne and the good folk of the village and their little dwellings and the parish church and the whole of Combray and of its surroundings, taking their proper shapes and growing solid, sprang into being, town and gardens alike, from my cup of tea.

II

Marcel Proust was born in 1871 around the beginning of *La Belle Époque*, an expression coined in the 1920's to describe Paris from the 1870's to the start of World War I in 1914. Proust's magnum opus *A la recherche du temps perdu* was published in seven volumes between 1913 and 1927, the last three volumes published posthumously. He died in 1922, the year Joyce's *Ullyses* and T.S.Eliot's *The Wasteland* were published.

Among the great novels of all times, Proust's work-- to borrow a phrase from Neruda-- is the most oceanic. I am talking here of, among others, Beckett's *Endgame*, Faulkner's *Absalom, Absolam*, Mann's *The Magic Mountain*, Joyce's *Ullyses* and Marquez' *Cien Años de Soledad*. Yet his *La Recherche* is the least read. The main reason for that is its incredible length. It is 3000 pages long, contains 1.5 million words and has 400 individual characters. Add to that, its longwinded style with sentences of 900 words that make its plot appear motionless. However, an immense patience and a deeper understanding of Proust's genius can transport the diligent reader to a massive world of art, music and painting. Then the labyrinthine words turn into a gigantic impressionistic fresco with a remarkable prose aria to boot.

> *George Piroue' has demonstrated in his brilliant study "Proust et la Musique du devenir" that this novel is written like a musical composition as if it was a symphony.*

We must appreciate that Proust was a writer between two centuries, the 19th and the 20th, between the realism of Balzac and Flaubert and the symbolism of Baudelaire and Mallarme. Can we then call Proust a modern novelist? He is modern because he finds redemption in art. Not love, not friendship, not worldly achievements but only through art –rather, only through the meditations to be found in art—that Proust finds a regaining of time, of recovering, re-possessing what is otherwise and always lost time.

It is usually remarked that *La Recherche* is a fictional autobiography of a man whose life mirrors Proust. Actually the novel is neither fiction nor a memoir. Nor is it a *roman a' clef.* It is an allegory of Proust's life, a creative autobiography so to speak. To Proust art is a translation of life. More to the point, it is a *roman-fleuve*, a series of novels acting as a commentary on an epoch, *La Belle Époch* when Paris was at the zenith of its artistic glory. In that golden age, the French capital was the center of the universe for all writers, painters and musicians and Proust knew most of them personally.

> *Clausewitz described war as continuation of policy by other means, Proust treated writing as continuation of life by other means. He was a megalomaniac of literature.*

It was the age of Nijinsky, La Boheme, absinthe and Can Can. Proust's novel is full of references to musicians Wagner and Debussy, writers Zola and Flaubert, painters Monet and Degas. The novel's world is the same world that was being painted by the impressionists. It was in this Parisian society that Proust encountered the figures upon whom he would model his characters. There was Comte Robert de Montesquiou, who became the repulsive Baron de Charlus; Sarah Bernhardt, who became the actress La Berma; Genevieve Strauss and the Comtesse Greffulhe, who were blended into the Duchesse de Guermantes. And so was the character of Swann based on Charles Haas and Charles Ephrussi. Proust heard the music of Saint-Saens and Cesar Frank, which would become Vinteuil's famous sonata and septet in the novel.

Living in that age of great music, Proust's novel came to possess a strong musical component. This musicality appears globally in the construction of his novel as well as in individual sentences. George Piroue' has demonstrated in his brilliant study *Proust et la Musique du devenir* that this novel is written like a musical composition as if it was a symphony. At the sentence level, just as the narrator borrows techniques from the painter Elstir, Proust is inspired by the musician Vinteuil and he composes his long sinuous sentences with an eye towards the aspects of classical music such as harmony, tune or recurrence.

Although this novel explores the philosophical themes of time, space and memory, it is above all a condensation of a wealth of literary, structural, stylistic and thematic possibilities. Being an omnivorous reader, Proust was educated in a wide range of subjects and his novel is replete with startlingly prescient insights into every aspect of the human condition from love and sex to religion and death. If you have seen the movie "Stealing Beauty" by Bertolucci I am sure, dear reader, you would have been haunted by that sentence by the dying gay writer played by Jeremy Irons: "L'incroyable frivolité de mourrant." (the incredible frivolity of the dying). I thought the scriptwriter, Susa Minot had coined that gem only to discover from Susan herself that I had mistook her for Proust!

III

In his own peculiar way, Proust was a theorist of time and space. *"An hour is not merely an hour, it is a vase full of scents and sounds and projects and climates"* he wrote. His novel, therefore in the final analysis, presents us with this dilemma. How should it be read? Is it literature or is it philosophy?

With a lesser writer combining literature and philosophy would undermine each other. But with Proust the whole is greater than the sum of the parts. Not only a coherent, distinctive philosophical system can be extracted from *La Recherche*, aspects of the aesthetic serve philosophical ends, enabling the reader to engage in an active manner with an alternative art of living.

We have all noticed going back to a favorite place in our childhood and discovered to our dismay that the old magic is gone. Why? Because what we remember is a place located not in physical space, but in time.

Clausewitz described war as continuation of policy by other means, Proust treated writing as continuation of life by other means. He was a megalomaniac of literature and literally shut himself in a room for fourteen years as he wrote his epic novel. He is reputed to write all night and sleep during the day. He belonged to four minorities of the *fin de siècle* Paris: Jew, homosexual, artist and the upper class. From age nine he suffered from asthma that drove him in-doors. Some of his biographers point out that he suffered from "hereditary neurasthenia" as a result of mixing two unusual parental strains: French catholic and Jewish. Thus the grammar of his life was loneliness that led to a complex sexual life and writing became a major part of his existence.

No wonder transience and time became the two major themes of his novel. (The comic sense of the absurd is the other.) The "self" is ever changing and so are people around us. Not just people but things and places change with time. Says Proust: "*Homes, avenues, roads, are, alas, as fugitive as years.*" We have all noticed going back to a favorite place in our childhood and discovered to our dismay that the old magic is gone. Why? Because what we remember is a place located not in physical space, but in time. It is not the magic of the remembered place that is lost, it is in fact the childhood's experience located in time that has been lost.

In his childhood, Proust lived in Illiers and Auteuil—both suburbs of Paris—but in his novel he invented a composite of the two and called it Combray. This imaginary place is what he remembers which is both mythical and universal and may remind readers of Marquez' *Macondo*, the mythic town of *Cien Años de Soledad*. While time transforms everything, in Combray nothing changes because it exists outside time. Like childhood, Combray becomes an idealized symbol of security in an uncertain world.

In the last volume of the novel "Time Regained," the narrator realizes that he is an old man ravaged by time. There is a sense of failure and futility. "*Trees*" he says "*you have no longer anything to say to me. My heart has grown cold and no longer hears you. If ever I thought of myself as a writer, I know now that I am not one.*"

Uttering these depressing words, he enters the memorable final party at the Guermantes mansion in Paris and suddenly experiences a series of epiphanies, flooding him with happiness. With the help of "Proustian memory" he regains his sense of wonder and confidence. He remembers the taste of tea and the Madeleine cookies; the smell of hawthorne bushes in bloom when he first met Gilbert, his first love; he remembers the subtle themes of the Vinteuil sonata, the spires at Martinville, the three trees near Balbec and all the other moments of joy from his past. He feels free now from the prison of time and once again, *experiences feelings of hunger, the desire for women, the pleasures of luxury, the blue volutes of the morning sea and, enveloped in them, phrases of music half emerging like the shoulders of water nymphs—the simplest act or gesture remains immured as within a thousand sealed vessels, each of them filled with things of a color, a scent, a temperature that are absolutely different one from another. But when our memory bridges the years with the smell or taste from one of these vessels it causes us suddenly to breathe a new air, an air which is new precisely because we have breathed it in the past, that purer air which the poets have vainly tried to situate in paradise and which could induce so profound a sensation of renewal only if it had been breathed before, since the true paradises are the paradises we have lost.*

With this final awareness, the narrator determines that the only purpose of his life is to recapture through writing those moments of paradise that have been lost.

Marcel Proust wrote in bed all night and slept all day.

Marcel Proust published the first part of his novel *Du côté de chez Swann* known in English as *Swann's Way* on November 14, 1913, exactly a 100 years ago. What is interesting is that he had to pay from his own pocket to publish his manuscript which is now regarded as the greatest Novel of the 20th century.

Gore Vidal - An American Iconoclast

President Kennedy and Gore Vidal sparring.

It is commonly believed that at age fourteen, Gore Vidal changed his name from Eugene Louis out of admiration for his grandfather, Senator T. P. Gore of Alabama. In reality the words *gore vidal* are Russian in origin and mean "he has seen grief." This anguish-ridden code name at such an early age shows Vidal's uncanny handling of his state of being gay in the convoluted world of the 1940's where being gay was either a crime, or worse, a disease that needed to be cured.

Vidal grew up in Washington DC in the sprawling home of his grandfather in Rock Creek Park. At age nineteen, he joined the US Navy and wrote his first novel *Williwaw* (a meteorological term for a sudden wind out of the mountain) which was widely praised. However, his third novel, *The City and the Pillar* written in 1948 began his life-long crusade against Puritanical America. This graphic coming of age story of the novel, rather what we now call a coming out story of a gay athlete, was demonized by even the then *New York Times* and blacklisted as corrupt and pornographic.

Eventually, Vidal wrote 25 novels and several plays for Broadway and screenplays for Hollywood including William Wyler's blockbuster, *Ben Hur*. But it was the essay form which suited his protean personality. Here he could be learned, witty, stylish. Here he could display his sophisticated cynicism about love, religion, patriotism, sex and above all the political and economic quagmire into which the American Republic had descended to. In more ways than one, he was another Montaigne, a truly American iconoclast.

> *Gore Vidal is reported to have said that it was Suetonius' book "Twelve Caesars" written around first century A.D. that persuaded him to be an essayist. He wanted to be remembered as an essayist who wrote the best sentences.*

Vidal was essentially an ancient. He was steeped in the classics as is evident from his Axial Age novel "Creation" which features, among others, Zoraster, Buddha, Mahavira, Confucius and Socrates. He is reported to have said that it was Suetonius' book "Twelve Caesars" written around first century A.D. that persuaded him to be an essayist. He wanted to be remembered as an essayist who wrote the best sentences:

"Because there is no cosmic point to the life that each of us perceives on this distant bit of dust at galaxy's edge, all the reason for us to maintain in proper balance what we have here. Because there is nothing else. No thing. That is it. And quite enough, all in all."

II

Over the last twenty years I have read and re-read Gore Vidal's 114 essays in his mammoth tome, *United States Essays 1952-1992*. It is interesting to note that Vidal read Screech's 1269 page translation of *The Complete Essays of Montaigne* in just one month. I, however, read his tome in a year and it co-incidentally consisted of 1271 pages just two more than Montaigne's! The book's separation into State of the Art, State of the Union, and State of Being, though arbitrary, gives us a clue into his three main passions: literary, political and personal.

Talking of his literary passion, Gore Vidal rarely attacked other writers. Mostly he criticized ideas and American culture. And chief among those was his indictment that America was *"the land of the dull and the home of the literal."* In this country, he said, our *"interests are mechanical, rather than imaginative...Never so happy as when changing a fan belt, Americans quite naturally want to communicate their joy in practical matters. The result has been depressing books of how-to-do things while works of literature are sternly rejected as not "practical" or "useful."*

In his book of essays, of course, he wrote about great literary figures like Montaigne or Tennessee Williams or E. L. Mencken or John Updike and treated them intimately as a close friend or colleague would. Above all, he turned the reader of his essays into a listener. Like a stand up comic he never failed to entertain with his irrepressible wit. Even when he is discussing a serious subject, there is always room for a *latifa* (joke). If incongruity is the soul of comedy, Vidal is a master. Who else could juxtapose Dr. Arthur Schlesinger as "Dr. Pendulum" in the midst of a scholarly discussion of "Monotheism and its Discontents?"

Nabokov's occasional commentaries were his favorite. Unlike him, Nabokov attacked celebrated authors like Hemingway and Conrad who wrote 'books for boys.' Nor could he tolerate "Mann's asinine *Death in Venice* or Pasternak's melodramatic and vilely written *Zhivago* or Faulkner's corn-cobby chronicles." It seems Vidal shares the delight of Nabokov in tearing apart *Don Quixote*, what he called a "cruel and crude old book." Or "that awful Monsieur Camus", or that "not quite first-rate Eliot…and definitely, second-rate Pound." However, he agrees with Nabokov's admiration of Borges, Joyce, Kafka and the first half of Proust's fairy tale *In Search of Lost Time*. Class dismissed.

> *"We are all growing old. That is the lesson of the street. Meanwhile what time is it? Daffodils, tulips and mimosa! What time is it? The same."*

Writing about himself, the question that Vidal most heard was why he spent almost a third of his life in an apartment in Rome? As he explains in his essay "At home in a Roman street," he just drifted into it. *"That's almost always the real answer to everything…Italo Calvino now lives at the north of the street, and we cher confrere one another when we meet. Then we move on…By and large the shops are exactly like the shops of two thousand years ago, as preserved at Pompeii..We are all growing old. That is the lesson of the street. Meanwhile what time is it? Daffodils, tulips and mimosa! What time is it? The same."*

III

Although Vidal never clearly mentions why he really abandoned America for Italy in the 1960's, it is clear that he was disgusted with *"the moral nullity at the heart of the American Empire."* America with its fascinating history of a truly democratic republic had now degenerated into a corrupt plutocracy in complete control of the state at every level. He laments that United States was a model for the world. But now it had turned into a joke and held in low regard. *"We are slipping into a police state and despotism, a militarized economy with armies marching into other countries."*

> **Truman established the "national security state" to fight the Cold War and since then the "predatory American eagle... constantly searches for external enemies to wage a permanent war in the name of permanent peace."**

In his many essays under the "political" sub-heading, he traces the birth of the American empire to 1893 with the *"liberation of Cuba and Philippines by American armies killing three million Filipinos, the largest single act of genocide until Hitler."* After the end of European empires during World War I and II, he writes, *"we created ours."* Truman established the *"national security state"* to fight the Cold War and since then the *"predatory American eagle... constantly searches for external enemies to wage a permanent war in the name of permanent peace."*

It was James Madison who said that *"the iron law of oligarchy always obtained in America."* No wonder the founding fathers coined the euphemism "pursuit of happiness" adds Vidal, *"which really means the pursuit of property."* This fundamental ambivalence in the US Constitution—where it was afraid both of true democracy as well as European monarchy—has finally ended in a plutocracy, a government of the rich, by the rich and for the rich. At the 1968 Republican Convention, Gore Vidal told William Buckley that there were no two political parties in the USA. There was only one political party, the "property" party. Democrats and Republicans were two right wings of the same party and beholden to the same corporate wealth. Is it any surprise that even the Supreme Court protects this oligarchy?

Given this world view, in a 1970 essay titled "How to Find God and Make Money" Vidal dealt with, for example, the illegal drug problem of the USA:

"Will anything sensible be done? Of course not. The American people are as devoted to the idea of sin and its punishment as they are to making money—and fighting drugs is nearly as big a business as pushing them. Since the combination of sin and money is irresistible (particularly to the professional politician), the situation will only grow worse."

Earlier in a 1963 essay "Edmund Wilson: Tax Dodger," Vidal explained:

"The truth is that the people of the United States are at present time dominated and driven by two kinds of officially propagated fear: fear of the Soviet Union and fear of the income tax: The result is a unique society in which we have free enterprise for the poor and socialism for the rich. The dazzling inequity is reflected in our tax system where the man on salary pays more tax than the man who lives on dividends, who in turn pays more tax than the wheeler-dealer who makes a capital gains deal...We have become a garrison state bemused by a rhetoric in which all is appearance, nothing reality."

As one reads these prescient words 50 years later in 2012, isn't it shocking how much they apply to the American society and politics of today. That is exactly what has happened after the Iraq War to oust Saddam on false pretexts, the 2008 economic collapse and the Occupy Wall Street movement as well as the nomination of a "wheeler-dealer" as the presidential candidate of the Republican Party! Romney not only refused to show all his back tax returns but himself admited to have paid only 13% maximum income tax on 2011 declared income of 41 million dollars, whereas his chauffer paid at least 25%.

> *Gore Vidal told William Buckley that there were no two political parties in the USA. There was only one political party, the "property" party. Democrats and Republicans were two right wings of the same party and beholden to the same corporate wealth.*

And yet some in the American media have called his essays "stark raving mad at how the land of the free is being subjugated under the iron heel of the evil corporate state." In a *Washington Post* article Peter Carlson wrote that "reading Vidal's long, rambling essay "The War at Home" is a little bit like watching a lovable but cranky old uncle drink too much at Thanksgiving and start bellyaching about the damn guv'mint." Vidal, always ready to respond to such criticism explained that present-day movie-star journalists who were paid movie-star salaries existed not to do any independent work *"but to serve the financial interests of their owners...However, the pure of heart can take some consolation in the fact that newspapers in America are less and less read."*

IV

Finally, turning to the "personal" essays, Gore Vidal own "state of being" drove him to change the discourse on sex and homosexuality incontrovertibly like no American writer before him. In his scathing essay "The Birds and the Bees" he demonstrated vividly that sexual attitudes of a given society are solely the result of political decisions. Therefore, *sex is politics*. "The dumb neologisms, homo-sexual and heterosexual," he wrote, "are adjectives that describe acts but never people." It was the dark ages that put a false stigma on homo-sexuality as "abnormal." He asserted quite correctly with the scientist Kinsey, that human beings are neither totally homo or totally hetro. Technically we are all bisexual:

> "The great unmentionable evil at the center of our culture is monotheism. From a barbaric Bronze Age text known as the Old Testament, three anti-human religions have evolved—Judaism, Christianity and Islam."

"From Plato to the rise of Pauline Christianity—which tried to put a lid on sex— man's variousness is explicit in classical writing. Yet to this day Christian, Freudian and Marxian commentators have all decreed or ignored this fact of nature in the interest each of a patented approach to the Kingdom of Heaven…Dr. Kinsey revealed in his dogged, arithmetical way that we are all a good deal less predictable and bland than anyone had suspected."

According to Vidal, the root cause of our ignorance of sex was the medieval religions that we follow. The same for our racism. In his classic essay, "Monotheism and its Discontents" he wrote:

"The great unmentionable evil at the center of our culture is monotheism. From a barbaric Bronze Age text known as the Old Testament, three anti-human religions have evolved—Judaism, Christianity and Islam. These are sky-god religions, where God is the omnipotent dictator, hence the loathing of women for 2,000 years by the earthly male delegates of that sky-god. Jewish men used to pray, 'I thank thee, Lord, that thou has not created me a woman.' Similarly… the hatred of blacks comes straight from the same book. As descendants of Ham (according to Redneck divines) blacks are forever cursed. Racism is in the marrow of the bone of the true believer."

In his authoritative essay "Sex and the Law" he brilliantly traces how puritanical laws became the law of this land. The Christian fundamentalists, he says, arrived in America not because they were persecuted in England for their religious beliefs but because they were forbidden to persecute others for *their* beliefs. (Reminds me of the contemporary Talibans of Afghanistan and the Wahabis of Saudi Arabia.) Thus, says Vidal, they made adultery and fornication criminal offenses in America even though no such laws existed in England. Unfortunately, these laws still exist on the books of 43 states in the USA, though thankfully they are seldom enforced. And then there are the dreaded miscegenation laws in 27 states forbidding sexual relations between the white race and its "inferiors:" blacks, American Indians and Orientals! With his characteristic wit, Gore Vidal concludes:

"This lunatic state of affairs could exist only in a society still obsessed by the puritanical code that the punishing of sin is the responsibility of the state...It is money, not sex, that Puritans want. After all, the English word for "coming" used to be "spending:" you spend your seed in woman's bank, and if the moon is right, nine months later you will get an eight pound dividend."

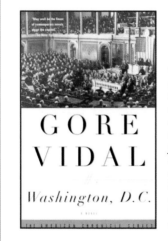

Washington, D.C., is the final installment in Gore Vidal's Narratives of Empire, his acclaimed six-volume series of historical novels about the American past. It offers an illuminating portrait of the republic from the time of the New Deal to the McCarthy era. Widely regarded as Vidal's ultimate comment on how the American political system degrades those who participate in it, Washington, D.C. is a stunning tale of corruption and diseased ambitions.

Esssay 13

Paul Gauguin's Sexual Dimorphism

Gauguin torn between Jesus and the Savage.

The life story of Gauguin is well known. Born in France in 1849, raised in Peru, a sailor in his twenties and a stockbroker after that. He was a collector of impressionist paintings of Pissarro and Degas and later in 1890 abandoned his family and financial career and became a notorious painter of the *fin de sieclè*.

We also know that he re-defined the art of painting. Unlike the impressionists he was never primarily interested in delicate effects of light; he preferred strong, hard and pungent colors and he was far more concerned with line, rhythm and arabesque. Nor did he submit passively to nature painting as practiced by his mentor Pissarro, still less to Monet where the sensation of the eye was paramount. For Gauguin, art was a reflection of the mind, of what he called the *centre mysterieux de la pensee* (mysterious center of thought). In his art, he proved the adage that only a genius could learn to paint like a child.

Like Delacroix he saw similarity between painting and music and in the overall musical effect of his canvas. He famously declared "My artistic center is in my own head and nowhere else." In his most ambitious painting which recast the book of genesis in Tahitian terms *Que sommes nous?* (Who are we?) painted before an attempt at suicide, all the landscape is blue and veronese green suggesting an escape from the literal as well as the negation of the realism of Monet and Renoir. This is truly painting as allegory, to quote Mallarmé "It is a musical poem and needs no libretto".

Art critics have also pointed out that Gauguin's quest for authenticity coupled with his originality contributed to the later art of Picasso and

Matisse. He was indeed a post-impressionist and offered a concrete stylistic alternative. The brevity, the bold simplicity and the vivid blocs of color of his paintings were a far cry from the more contemplative and detailed art of the Impressionists. "He made painting itself into such a sacred act" wrote Francoise Cachin, "that the liberties he took with it ultimately led to modern art for it was the painting that became the absolute truth, not life." In a letter to Van Gogh, Gauguin remarked: "I feel I have been right about art."

> *Unlike the impressionists Gauguin was never primarily interested in delicate effects of light; he was far more concerned with line, rhythm and arabesque. For Gauguin, art was a reflection of the mind, of what he called the* **centre mysterieux de la pensee** *(mysterious center of thought).*

It is also well known that he, more than any of his contemporaries, hated the industrial civilization of the 19th century. It is said that he was in love with the primitive, the archaic and the unspoiled. His fascination of distant lands is traced by biographers to his childhood voyages to Peru and later to *Valparaiso* in Chile as a sailor. This search for earthly paradise became his life-long quest that first took him to Brittany, then to Martinique and finally to Tahiti and the Marquesas islands.

What is seldom explained, however, is why did he escape into the primitive? What motivated him to search for the earthly paradise in which invariably he depicted himself in painting after painting as the "fallen angel." Why did he indulge in mythmaking? What was this life-long quest for authenticity? Nor has it been made clear that the primitive or the savage for Gauguin was opposed to the modern in complex ways: in the conceptions of sex, nature, property rights and family life. In all these domains the primitive, as he understood it, was different from the perceived wisdom of European civilization.

II

In a recent study of the science of gender, it is now clearly understood that, at best, gender is ambiguous. Take, for example, what is known on the Indian subcontinent as *hijra*. This human is neither male nor female.

The most striking feature of a hijra is that his genitals are most difficult to define. Some even possess both male and female organs. These individuals are now called inter-sex in the West. Many inter-sex people today see themselves not male or female but in-between, some form of a third sex. To complicate matters you have transgenders. Whereas a transvestite is a person who is a crossdresser, a transgender's sex is driven by the mind. Here it is a male who feels a female inside and vice versa.

It is my contention that Gauguin's life story and his rebellious art was the result of his gender ambiguity. In one of his famous remarks he said: "I am myself a woman." Although in his revised book *Noa Noa* he argued that sexual dimorphism is not natural but cultural --he obviously was mistaken-- today scientists are convinced that gender variation in humans is natural just as plants and animal kingdom are at least 1/3rd hermaphrodite. Modern scientific studies have actually shown that the frequency of inter-sex in humans is 1 in 250. As a matter of fact there is heterosexual sex at one end of the spectrum and homosexual sex on the other extreme. In between these two poles is infinite variation of gender liminality almost impossible to quantify.

> *The concept of an androgynous being --deified in Tahitian mythology as* **Mahu-** *- is a recurring symbol in most of Gauguin's paintings from* **Matamua** *(old times) to* **Mahana no atua** *(day of God) to his masterpiece* **D'ou venons nous?** *(Where do we come from?)*

Nevertheless, from the moment Gauguin set foot on Tahiti in 1891 he was not only called an eccentric Symbolist painter but was renamed *taata vahine* (man-woman) by the natives. The term taata vahine was the local designation for a transvestite although it could also have meant transgender. This concept of an androgynous being --deified in Tahitian mythology as *Mahu*-- is a recurring symbol in most of Gauguin's paintings from *Matamua* (old times) to *Mahana no atua* (day of God) to his masterpiece *D'ou venons nous?* (Where do we come from?)

The ethnographer and diplomat Jacques Moerenhout describes the mystical union of Tahitian gods *Ta'aroa* (male) and *Hina* (female) into a single androgynous power. For Gauguin this union became the omnipresent Polynesian god. "The earth is a garment" wrote Balzac. Gauguin might add "So is Sex." Understanding the *Mahu* as a result of Tahitian culture, Gauguin became very interested in Tahitian lore and mythology. After reading Moerenhout on the subject of gender liminality, in which the separateness of male and female disappeared, he began writing his own treatise *Ancien Culte Mahorie*. In this way, in due course, race, sex and gender became the main concern of Gauguin's art. To that iconoclastic vision he added the complexities of colonial identity in his later years.

In Tahiti, Gauguin not only mythologized himself but he mythologized the island itself to fit his own ends. All his guises, Gauguin the lost soul on a spiritual quest, Gaugin the martyr, Gaugin the evil Lucifer, the fallen angel and finally Gaugin the savage, the embodiment of a primitive consciousness was obviously a coping mechanism with his own sexual dialectic. Gradually he moved away from painting life as he saw it. As an artist, he did not want to be a realist or copy nature. Instead he wanted to paint images and ideas forged in his mind. He therefore replaced the natural world with colors of a dreamscape, a Tahitian utopia where race and sex were combined in a "primitive communism" where land and its resources belonged to all.

His 1892 painting *Te nave nave fuena* (The Delightful Land) depicts a portrait which is neither European nor Tahitian, neither black or white, neither Venus or chimpanzee. It is actually a liminal character. In the words of Levi Strauss, the post-existentialist French philosopher and author of "The Structural Study of Myth," here we can see the structural mental basis of mythic thought. In his paintings, Gauguin provides the genesis mythology of Tahitian hybrid identity. For this we have to see his 1893 painting *Merahi matua no Tehamana* (Tehmana has many parents) which is a portrait of the Tahitian Eve. Tahiti thus provided Gauguin with a mélange of cultures and mulatto races which held a great erotic fascination for him.

Along with sex and race, Gauguin's paintings also depicted the complexity of colonial identity. He saw Polynesian women like Parisian prostitutes and Tahitian queens. They sit, stand, walk, swim, sing, dance, pray, sleep and dream. Men are less often depicted than women but when they are, they display a gender ambiguity that reveal some uniquely Tahitian sexual verities.

As was explained earlier, particularly fascinating in Gauguin's mythmaking was his dimorphic view of sex. For him Tahiti highlighted a multitude of genders. In the Western Pacific he saw sex less an identity than a means of understanding the world. Western civilization keeps women clothed and artificially weak physically whereas the naked women in Tahiti did all kinds of physical labor and were more like men. In his painting *Mana' o tupapa'u* (The Specter watches over her) he shows a virile woman with sexual desire as real and palpable as a man's. On the other hand, his men

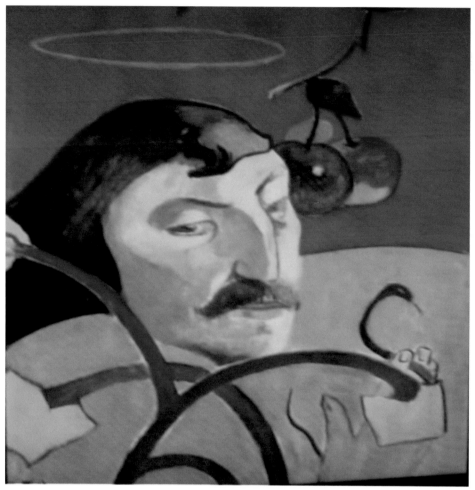

Self-Portrait: Gauguin as Lucifer.

are repeatedly shown as feminine thus giving rise to his concept of the third sex or *inverti* as known in France –Paul Verlaine and Oscar Wilde being the famous examples--or Mahu in the Tahitian lore.

This worldview was anti-colonial because as Edward Said wrote in his admirable book "Culture and Imperialism" the essence of western imperialism was the "male power fantasy." Nevertheless, on the island of Hiva-Oa, Gauguin built a temple of his erotic and savage faith and called it *Maison de Plaisir* (House of Pleasure). There he lived a life of art, libertinage and political agitation. Joseph Martin, the catholic bishop on the island persuaded the colonial authorities to charge the "bestial and degenerate" Gauguin with sedition. Gauguin retorted by wickedly caricaturing the bishop in a sculpture called "Father Lechery," which depicted the priest as a giant phallus.

In 1903 Gauguin was convicted of libel and sentenced to three months in jail. Gauguin, however, died of syphilis before he could be put in jail. He was 54 years old. The Marquesan "Self Portrait" was his last and best work. It was retrospective and funereal, modeled in part after late Roman funerary portraits from Fayum and Thebes. In it he resembled Lucifer, the fallen angel, who failed to find his earthly paradise. Playfully painted, in this caricature, halo intact and framed by the apples of temptation, he is seen grasping the serpent.

All his guises, Gauguin the lost soul on a spiritual quest, Gaugin the martyr, Gaugin the evil Lucifer, the fallen angel and finally Gaugin the savage, the embodiment of a primitive consciousness was obviously a coping mechanism with his own sexual dialectic

Esssay 14

Carlos Fuentes and the Alphabet of the Human Condition

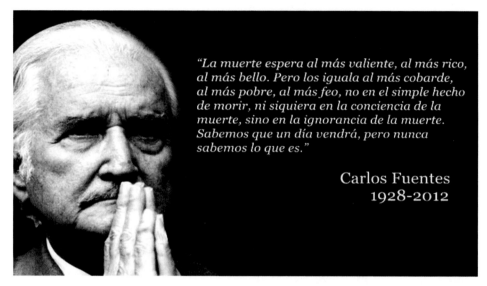

"La muerte espera al más valiente, al más rico, al más bello. Pero los iguala al más cobarde, al más pobre, al más feo, no en el simple hecho de morir, ni siquiera en la conciencia de la muerte, sino en la ignorancia de la muerte. Sabemos que un día vendrá, pero nunca sabemos lo que es."

Carlos Fuentes
1928-2012

Death awaits the most courageous, the richest, the most beautiful. But it makes equal the most coward, the poorest and the ugliest, not in the simple act of dying, not even in the consciousness of death, but in the ignorance of it. We know that one day it will come, but never know what it is.

Novelist, essayist, scholar and diplomat Carlos Fuentes was one of the world's foremost international literary figures. In the last five decades Fuentes wrote 20 books whose magnitude and enormity is breathtaking. He defined, among other things, the cultural and emotional identity of the Spanish speaking world.

The son of a Mexican diplomat, Fuentes spent most of his childhood in Washington DC later to become Mexico's ambassador to France. He subsequently inaugurated the Robert F. Kennedy chair in Latin American studies at Harvard and has been the Simon Bolivar Professor at Cambridge. He was a visiting professor at Princeton and professor at large at Brown University.

After a superb sense of irony, paradox and sensuality which pervades his novels — *Terra Nostra, The Old Gringo, The Death of Artemio Cruz* — Fuentes turned his considerable erudition to philosophical reflections in his book *This I Believe: An A to Z of a Life.* An anthology of 40 essays arranged alphabetically from "Amore" to "Zurich," *This I Believe* explores what Arthur Schlesinger has called "the alphabet of the human condition." This passionate memoir — which is both a biography and an autobiography — surveys the wellsprings of art and ideology as well as a deeply personal inner journey of a prolific and truly liberal writer.

> *An anthology of 40 essays arranged alphabetically from "Amore" to "Zurich," "This I Believe" explores what Arthur Schlesinger has called "the alphabet of the human condition."*

Brilliantly translated from Spanish into English by Kristina Cordero, this book is an elegant and lyrical meditation on abundantly varied topics. From the mixed curse and blessings of globalization to the encounters with the devastation and hope of revolutions; from the transformational power of love to the clash between history and civil society; from a celebration of literary writers like Balzac, Cervantes, Faulkner, Kafka and Shakespeare to his favorite film directors, including his life-long friend Luis Buñuel; from sex, beauty, friendship and death to God. Meditating on the ecstasies of sex, he declares that the end of sexual relationship was the time when sex could be transformed into literature. "A body of words crying out for the closeness of another body of words."

To say that Fuentes is a truly civilized and an eclectic individual is to state the obvious. Witness these few quotes from his essays:

"*Don Quixote* contains both the question and the answer. It is a modern novel with multiple points of view that live in active dialogue with itself. In Spain that exiled half of itself when it expelled the Jews in 1492 and the Moors in 1603, this work of Cervantes is a paradox of a paradox." ("Quixote")

"Culture is a product of many races and many traditions. We are all descendants of Greeks and Romans, Arabs and Jews. We must examine those roots to discover who we are today." ("Zebra")

"Politics can be dogmatic. The novel can only be enigmatic." ("Novel")

"What the United States does best is to understand itself. What it does worse is to understand others."

"Jesus did not resurrect the dead. He revived the living. Jesus is the copy editor of human life."("Christ")

"Faulkner rejects the foundations of American Dream and tells his countrymen that we too can fail. We too can bear the cross of tragedy. This cross is called racism." ("Faulkner")

Finally, his fierce indictment of the contemporary Religious Right in the USA: "Witness today the re-emergence of fascism, anti-Islamism, anti-Latin-Americanism-all of them violent forms of Xenophobia and hostility towards "The Other" or all that is different. Homophobia, misogyny, racism." ("Xenophobia")

> *"What the United States does best is to understand itself. What it does worse is to understand others."*

Without naming names, in an obvious jab at the Bush administration, Fuentes concluded his essay on "Politics" as follows: "I am concerned about the barbaric stance of preventive war. I am concerned by the diversion of fight against terrorism to the selective overthrowing of tyrants if they happen to sit on barrels of oil."

If I had to choose my favorite essays in *This I Believe*, they would be "Silvia" and "Urbanites". "Silvia" is a short essay on Fuentes' wife who imparts to him a great lesson of life: "Pay attention" she says "or you will not have the right to love me and be loved by me." Fuentes adds: "A couple may never know which one will outlive the other. Eroticism is the approval of life, even in death. "

The best pages in this book are in the essay titled "Urbanites" where Fuentes evokes the streets, cafes and bedrooms of major cities of his life like Washington DC, Mexico, Santiago de Chile, Venice, London, Prague and New York to name a few. But it is Paris for which he has deeply emotional words:

"I adore the cities that instead of burying and hiding themselves away, stretch out, show themselves off, expose their spaces like jewels spread out on a velvet. Paris changes but does not hide. It expands but does not disappear. Those of us who are inveterate lovers of this city can bemoan the disappearance of a bookshop, a cafe, a market. But in its essence, Paris does not change."

If there is a small shortcoming in Fuentes' book, it is the usual grandiloquence common to several Latin American writers. But it is in his flights of fancy that one imagines the romance of language and ideas. After all as he himself put it, "We remain decrepit, ruined prisoners of the last great cultural revolution, which was romanticism."

This I Believe is a book full of enduring thoughtful pleasures. It is a book that Goethe termed *"Weltliteratur"* or 'universal world literature.'

I adore the cities that instead of burying and hiding themselves away, stretch out, show themselves off, expose their spaces like jewels spread out on a velvet. Paris changes but does not hide. It expands but does not disappear.

Esssay 15

Global Gilded Age

You can never be too rich or too thin.
---Duchess of Windsor.

As I write this essay in June 2013, the world is witnessing a summer of uprising and discontent worldwide. From Cairo's Tahrir Square to Sao Paulo's Paulista Avenue to Istanbul's Taksim Square, throngs of frustrated new middle class individuals are protesting not merely for economic survival but about their quality of life compared to the affluent, authoritarian and mostly corrupt leaderships. Taking cue from the Occupy Movement in the US and Spain's *indignados*, the rage of the unemployed is brewing against Capitalism.

Twenty years ago, in 1993, I wrote an essay called "Liberal Democracy, Free Market and the Other Voice" which looking back, was a mild indictment of the Capitalist Markets of that era. 'Capitalism' I wrote, had no goal. It's sole purpose was to produce more. It knows all about prices but nothing about values.' It was obvious to any student of history that Capitalism and Inequality were always in conflict with each other. However, in the US one hoped that with the creation of the modern welfare state by FDR and later improved by LBJ that capitalism and democracy could co-exist in relative harmony.

Ten years later, in 2003, I pursued the same subject in a book review of Kevin Phillips' *Wealth and Democracy*. From J.P.Morgan to Bill Gates, Phillips meticulously traced the phases of wealth concentration and the politics of the Plutocrats in which the USA found itself gripped by the rule of Wall Street and multi-national corporations. By 2003 the wealthiest one percent of American households owned more than 40% of all assets higher than any year since 1929.

Little did one know, that the dawn of the 21st century not only ushered 9/11 and two tragic and wasteful wars, but it also saw a global gilded age bloom. Between 2002 and 2007, 65% of all income growth in the U.S. went to the richest 1% of the population. Today, in spite of the *Great Recession*, half of the national income goes to the richest 10%. In 2007, the top 1% controlled 34.6% of the wealth—significantly more than the bottom 90% who controlled just 26.9%.

Income inequality is also increasing globally and now is as high in China as in the U.S. Witness for example the remnants of China's *hukou* system of household registration which curtails social mobility and thus perpetuates poverty. In varying degrees the same phenomenon is repeating itself in India, Mexico, Russia, the U.K. and many other countries. For details see Chrystia Freeland's facts-filled book *Plutocrats: The Rise of the New Global Super Rich and the Fall of Everyone Else.*

In the USA, the top 1% controlled 34.6% of the wealth—significantly more than the bottom 90% who controlled just 26.9%.

As readers of history know, it was Mark Twain who called the last three decades of the 19th century the "Gilded Age." By this he meant that the period was glittering on the surface but corrupt beneath. Like the Gilded Age of yore, we live in a time when almost everything can be bought and sold. Market thinking so permeates our lives in this global gilded age, that we barely notice it anymore. A leading US philosopher Michael Sandel sums up the hidden costs of this *price tag society* in a shocking Atlantic Monthly article published in April 2012. Today the so-called free market—where we have drifted from a market economy to a market society—seeps into every aspect of human endeavor and even social relations are made over in the image of the market. The logic of capitalism seems to transform everything.

A similar corrosion of values has occurred in Asia's own contemporary gilded age where money has become a measure of all things and vast riches seem to redeem intellectual and emotional inadequacies. In the early 20th century, writers like Sinclair Lewis (*Main Street*) and Scott Fitzgerald (*The Great Gatsby*) laid bare that cash nexus in the West but not many western fiction writers dwell on that topic anymore. In Asia, on the other hand, novelists like the Pakistani Mohsin Hamid (*How to Get Filthy Rich in Rising Asia*), the Malaysian Tash Aw (*Five Star Billionaire*) and the Sri Lankan Randy Boyagada (*Beggar's Feast*) examine the perils of Asian capitalism and the sudden glorification of greed which for centuries had been criticized by conventional religions and philosophies. Since the fall of Lehman Brothers in 2008 and the subsequent crash of the housing market almost in every country of the planet, however, a plethora of books by economists like Stiglitz (*The Price of Inequality*) or journalists like Michael Lewis (*The Big Short*) and movies (*Wall Street* or *Margin Call*) have appeared dealing with the financial and economic catastrophe.

In my view, before 1980, barring some third world countries, the middle class and the rich –all over the world— grew together. After 1980 and Reagan, beginning in the USA, the divide got bigger and bigger and then spread globally, not to say that some feudal third world societies had already an endemic inequality of their own. No doubt, starting with the 1990's, the twin forces of globalization and technical innovation have actually narrowed inequality globally, as poorer countries and emerging market economies have caught up with richer

> *A similar corrosion of values has occurred in Asia's own contemporary gilded age where money has become a measure of all things and vast riches seem to redeem intellectual and emotional inadequacies.*

ones, but within many of these third world countries, income gaps and wealth have recently also widened. Although nearly one billion of the extremely poor have moved out of endemic poverty in the last 30 years –75% of those are in China-- most of the third world leaders (much like the US *winner-take-all society*) would rather sweep the issue of inequality under the rug.

In China credit is siphoned to state owned enterprises and well connected insiders; the elite also gain from a string of monopolies. In the Russia the oligarchs' wealth has even less to do with being entrepreneurs. In India too its leaders refuse to tackle deep-rooted corruption. In Korea, monopolies completely dominate the economy. On the other hand, Latin American emerging economies have done, by and large, a better job in controlling inequality by investing in poor schools and pioneered conditional cash transfers for the very poor (eg: Brazil's *Bolsa Familia*), although these countries still dole out unaffordable pensions to the already affluent families with military connections. Nevertheless during the last twenty years (according to a recent study by The World Bank) owing to economic mobility some 150 million Latin Americans have moved from poverty to the middle class and an equal number now belong to lower middle class, which is not extremely poor.

II

I believe it was Alexis de Tocqueville who warned in 1830 that unless the 'general equality of condition among the people' -- which was the bedrock of American democracy -- was maintained, democracy would not survive. The danger he saw was the increasingly economic inequality that would subvert democracy. Today, the gap between "masters" and "workmen" has widened beyond anything he could have envisioned.

The Hamptons of New York and Washington DC's chic suburbs offer two venues of the most striking characteristic of American inequality: the surge in wealth at the top.

The Hamptons of New York and Washington DC's chic suburbs offer two venues of the most striking characteristic of American inequality: the surge in wealth at the top. Washington's *superzips* as they are called are full of the rich: people in the top 5% of the income distribution earning more than $340,000 a year. The helicopter passengers in the Hamptons epitomize America's ultra-wealthy, the top 0.01%, with an annual income of $8m or more. Over the past 30 years incomes have soared both among the wealthy and the ultra-wealthy. The result has been a huge, and widening, gap—financially, socially and geographically—between America's elite and the rest of the country. Today the middle class in America which used to be 61% of the population in 1970 has shrunk below 50% in 2013.

A disproportionate and growing chunk of the very rich have made their money in Wall Street rather than Main Street. America's top 25 hedge-fund managers make more than all the CEOs of the S&P 500 combined. Goldman Sachs, the premier Wall Street investment bank, whose subsidiary a wag has quipped is the US Treasury department, has been described by the Rolling Stone journalist Matt Taibbi as a "great vampire squid wrapped around the face of humanity, relentlessly jamming its blood funnel into anything that smells like money." Senator Carl Levin described Goldman Sachs as a "financial snake pit." The bathos is palpitating when Blankfien the CEO of the firm told The Times of London that he was "doing God's work."

On the other side of the debate, Senator Elizabeth Warren of Massachusetts aptly remarks that after the crash of 2008, not a single Wall Street investment banker went to jail: " *Ordinary people feel like the system is rigged against them… And here is the painful part: they are right. The system is rigged. Look around. Oil companies guzzle down billions in subsidies. Billionaires pay lower tax rates than their secretaries. Wall Street CEO's –the same ones who wrecked our economy and destroyed millions of jobs—strut around Congress, no shame, demanding favors and acting like we should thank them. Anyone here have a problem with that? Well I do.*"

And that is the crux of the whole matter. The long and painful decline of the middle class in this age of greed is not a result of so-called "free market forces" but of manipulation of the political process. It is a direct consequence of the incestuous relationship that exists between economic oligarchs of Manhattan with the political oligarchy of DC. We now have a financial aristocracy that controls the US government. Money now plays an ever bigger role in politics, goes the argument, so the clout of the ultra-wealthy grows, particularly to block things they don't like.

Without trying to over-argue my view, witness today the likes of the Koch brothers who buy not only the US government but they also buy public opinion thus deluding a taxi driver I met in El Paso, Texas who said that the rich are the "job creators" and we need to cut their taxes so that more jobs are created! The propaganda machine financed by the super rich, namely the Fox News channel, talks relentlessly about budget deficits and national

> *The long and painful decline of the middle class in this age of greed is not a result of so-called "free market forces" but of manipulation of the political process.*

debt. No body talks of the trade deficits, which have been going wrong for the US for the last 37 years. Why? Because US based multinationals import their foreign manufactured goods free of any duties. As a result the US is one of the largest debtor nations owing trillions to China and Japan, among others. But has Fox News ever discussed that global imbalance that is the root cause of recent global financial and housing credit booms and busts?

With a few exceptions, the western media has done a lousy job in highlighting inequality. Similarly, it has misunderstood and misinterpreted the so-called two decades of economic malaise in Japan. From the point of view of dealing with inequality Japan has done a much better job than the rest of the West. In a recent article, Nobel laureate Stiglitz says: *Those who see Japan's performance over the last decades as an unmitigated failure have too narrow a conception of economic success. Along many dimensions — greater income equality, longer life expectancy, lower unemployment, greater investments in children's education and health, and even greater productivity relative to the size of the labor force — Japan has done better than the United States. It may have quite a lot to teach us. If Abenomics is even half as successful as its advocates hope, it will have still more to teach us.*

III

The contrast in fortunes between those on top of the economy and those buried in the rubble can't be starker. In the US, the 10 largest banks today control more than 75% of banking assets. Since these banks are now "too big to fail," with the help of the Federal Reserve policies of zero interest rates for the last 5 years, profits have bounced back on Wall Street where the stock market has recovered 11 trillion dollars for its rich shareholders since the low of March 2009.

This is happening at a time when millions of middle class homeowners live in homes that are "under water." Twenty four million Americans are unemployed or under-employed and since 2008 nine trillion in middle class household wealth has vanished. There seems to be no correlation between who drove the crisis of 2008 and who is paying the price. Pity the Obama administration whose every effort to tackle inequality has been successfully blunted by the rich run Republican opposition. Pity also the middle class savers of America who played by the rules and given the callous Federal Reserve policies have been robbed of $635 billion of interest income in the last four years, according to Moneyrates.com.

Needless to say, the political oligarchy has no interest in looking after the middle class. The callousness of the affluent is alarming in spite of the shocking trend among white middle class baby boomers whose suicide rates according to *The Washington Post* have shot up precipitously between 1999 and 2010. The Tea Party looked like a populist movement but when we saw its true face it was not a movement of average Americans. It is clearly a Trojan horse planted by the rich to blunt any genuine populist movement. Their peculiar agenda is to slash the size of government without touching tax breaks for corporations and the wealthy. In short, the US has moved in political terms from a broad populism to a narrow plutocracy.

Over the past decade, the US and several other economies have squandered—with the exception perhaps of emerging markets—trillions of dollars on rampant leveraged speculation to the tune of 40 to 1, rather than making investments in technology, infrastructure, education and clean energy that could have alleviated the plight of the middle class. On Wall Street we have a new fad called *High Frequency Trading* which led on May 6, 2010 to the so-called FLASH CRASH when the Dow fell nearly 1000 points in 5 minutes. This algorithmic trading is done by only 2% of the traders but it controls 75% of all daily trades in the US financial markets. It is hard to believe that world stock markets are now high tech casinos where microseconds matter and an average stock is "held" for 22 seconds!

Given the current Global Financial state of affairs can we still get history and the future right? As they say time is running out. The 'cult of Money' that Pope Francis decried in May 2013 will be hard to reverse. *"The rich are always with us…they are different from you and me"* said Bette Davis in a film released in the teeth of the Great Depression. Almost 80 years later, in a movie called *"Arbitrage,"* the actress Susan Sarandon echoes the same emotion: *"How much money do you need?"* she tells her Hedge Fund Manager husband. *"Do you want to be the richest man in the cemetery?"*

On the other hand, it must also be said that no doubt the first Gilded Age was an era of corruption, conspicuous consumption and unfettered capitalism with American robber barons and Europe's "Downton Abbey," but the fear of a socialist revolution spawned a wave of reforms from Theodore Roosevelt's trust-busting to Lloyd George's People's Budget. In early 20th century, western Governments promoted competition, introduced progressive taxation and wove the first threads of a social safety net, later to be dubbed as "The New Progressive Era."

> *It is hard to believe that world stock markets are now high tech casinos where microseconds matter and an average stock is "held" for 22 seconds!*

As we examine the complexity of that era we might consider whether there is a creative subtext to our own Global Gilded Age. May be we are on the verge of another "Progressive Era"? But at the moment the signs are not good. There is gridlock in Washington. The conservatives are still not convinced that inequality matters. Leaders like Speaker Boehner, instead of blaming the real culprits of the recent meltdown, blame big government, which is a proxy for cutting social security and Medicare. The Democrats under Obama are caught up in their own purist position that all will be well if they can raise income tax rates on the wealthy and increase spending by piling on more debt. Needless to say, the Obama administration has lacked the political skills to outmaneuver the Republicans.

In a 2012 Special Report on the World Inequality, *The Economist* proposed several bold steps harking back to the 1910 Osawatomie Speech by Theodore Roosevelt, from trust busting in India and China to removing subsidies for too-big-to fail banks, rebuilding infrastructure and tax reforms in the U.S. Strange to say, according to *The Economist* parts of the agenda are already taking shape in emerging economies like Brazil, China, India and Indonesia whereas the most shocking dysfunction still remains in the U.S. Congress. President Obama gave his own version of the Osawatomie speech in 2012 after winning re-election, declaring "inequality as the defining issue of our time." But his proposals for raising top income tax rate marginally to increasing college tuition subsidies were pathetically small initiatives. Roosevelt would have been shocked by his timidity. May be a bolder and politically more experienced President in the near future like a Hillary Clinton may usher a desperately needed new Progressive Era. At least one can hope.

Article 1

An Evening with Mohsin Hamid at Politics and Prose

Mohsin Hamid and the late Carla Cohen at Politics and Prose in Washington DC. (April 2007)

In late April, Mohsin Hamid's brilliant second novel "The Reluctant Fundamentalist" was the object of regard at the renowned Washington D.C. bookstore "Politics and Prose".

Some three hundred book lovers— at least a quarter of them of South Asian origin—crowded the book shop, most with a copy of the novel in hand, to get it autographed by the esteemed writer.

This was Hamid's twelfth stop on an ongoing hectic book tour that made him criss-cross the entire American continent, from sea to shining sea, perhaps, with not enough sleep in between. The atmosphere created in the book shop with overflowing admirers reminded me of the hilarious Dylan Thomas poem "A Visit to America" which reads, in part:

"Across the United States of America /From New York to California /And back glazed again / For many months of the year /There streams and sings for its heady supper /A dazed and prejudiced procession of foreign lecturers /Scholars, sociologists, economists, writers / Authorities on this and that /And, even in theory on the United States of America…"

The proceedings began with Carla Cohen, the co-owner of the popular bookshop, introducing Hamid in glowing terms. She called the novel very well written and "haunting." Our novelist then started his presentation by reading an excerpt from his first novel, "Moth Smoke" which he called a mirror image of "The Reluctant Fundamentalist". He followed this by reading three excerpts from his latest work, interspersed with provocative comments.

Listening to him, one could not help being impressed by this Pakistani prodigy. Not only is his writing imbued with a sophistication and maturity of a great talent but he also spoke with an equally canny intelligence and command of nuance.

Hamid explained that his new work was not a traditional, one dimensional Immigrant's novel but an Emigrant's novel, where his protagonist, Changez comes to America, falls in love and then gets disillusioned after 9/11, before returning to Lahore, his hometown. More on this later.

> *Listening to Mohsin Hamid, one could not help being impressed by this Pakistani prodigy. Not only is his writing imbued with a sophistication and maturity of a great talent but he also spoke with an equally canny intelligence and command of nuance.*

Hamid went on to elucidate that although his novel was a slim one, it took seven drafts and seven years to complete. No wonder he felt that this long gestation period was like giving birth to a pearl. Kind of reminded me of Bharati Mukherjee's comment from one of her novels that she is "really incubating an enormous diamond."

The reason it took so long to write this novel, he said, was his search for the precise voice for the single person narration of his protagonist. After several drafts, he decided on a voice that was "courtly and menacing, a vaguely anachronistic voice rooted in the Anglo-Indian heritage of elite Pakistani schools and suggestive of an older system of values and of an abiding historical pride."

As a result, when he finished the sixth draft in early 2006, Simon Prosser at Hamish Hamilton in U.K. bought it right away. Later, he worked with him and another agent, who bought it for Harcourt in America, followed by a seventh revision.

This detailed explanation of the process made it clear how much effort, time, money and team-work go into the making of a marketable work of fiction in the West.

Next, Hamid dealt with the question of how politicians or even journalists invariably simplify complex issues. For example, labels like "Axis of Evil" or "Islamo-fascism" are not only reductive, but they are absurd. The conflict between East and the West, he said, was the result of mutual ignorance and suspicion. The crucial issue was "an empathy deficit" between the two sides.

It is this theme of suspicion between the two worlds that Hamid says he played upon in his novel. You have a bearded Muslim man, Changez, who is like a chameleon constantly changing his moods. He tells his life story to a mysterious American stranger who is, perhaps, armed and may be even an assassin. At one point, he says:

"I hope you will not mind my saying so, but the frequency and purposefulness with which you glance about brings to mind the behavior of an animal that has ventured too far from its lair and is now in unfamiliar surroundings, uncertain whether it is predator or prey!"

In my view, this paradox of who is the predator and who is the prey is the central pivot of Hamid's novel on which he works his magic, subtly. Those of us who have read Orhan Pamuk's novel "Snow" will recall a somewhat similar encounter between a Turkish fundamentalist and a liberal professor in a café in Kars. In the end the fundamentalist murders the professor. On the other hand, most readers are aware how meetings with fundamentalists in Karachi cafes resulted in the execution/murder of an American journalist, Daniel Pearl.

> *In my view, this paradox of who is the predator and who is the prey is the central pivot of Hamid's novel on which he works his magic, subtly. Those of us who have read Orhan Pamuk's novel "Snow" will recall a somewhat similar encounter between a Turkish fundamentalist and a liberal professor in a café in Kars. In the end the fundamentalist murders the professor.*

Mohsin Hamid talked for about twenty minutes and then invited questions from the audience.

The first question I asked him about his novel was whether he would agree that his characters of Erica and Chris were more allegorical than real persons because they were very thinly drawn sketches. Besides, Changez's capricious love for America mirrored his affair with Erica. In fact at a crucial juncture in the novel both America and Erica are shown to suffer from a dangerous "nostalgia." Was it a co-incidence that the name "Erica" rhymed with "America" or that Erica's dead former lover, Chris appeared to be a metaphor for Christianity?

Hamid gave a short, non-committal reply. He said that his novel was not an allegory and that it was a love story, both with America and a woman by the name of Erica. I don't blame him for saying so since the other interpretation would transform his novel into a didactic work and move the narrative from drama to an essay.

My second question to Hamid was regarding his classification of "The Reluctant Fundamentalist" as an Emigrant's not an Immigrant's novel. I asked if the real reason for Changez's departure from America was not the aftermath of 9/11 alone, but as he himself put it in the novel "I was, in four and half years never an American."

As we know from the novel, Changez had no mainstream friends in America. The only two friends he had were presumably an African American and a gay person. Further, Changez detested his fellow employees at his firm who invariably acted as the world's "ruling class."

Under these circumstances, his epiphany while in Chile, that he was a "modern-day janissary" was it not an over-reaction born of his own insecurities? I asked.

Hamid disagreed with the thrust of my question and explained how many Pakistanis of his generation who had lived in New York for less than 10 years got truly disgusted with the treatment of Muslims after 9/11 and therefore quit. Immigrants living in America for over 10 years did stay on, he said.

I agreed with Hamid that no doubt some Muslims were singled out and harshly discriminated against prompting even Philip Roth to write a novel titled "Plot against America" but hopefully the immediate American paranoia to the 9/11 attacks would be only a passing phase in U.S. political history. As we have seen, after the recent 2006 general elections, the bogus xenophobia orchestrated by the Cheney-Bush policies was already unraveling. Today, all Americans had begun to suffer from 9/11 fatigue.

Having lived in the USA for thirty years, I added, what I believe will endure for first generation immigrants like Changez is the age-old question which I raised in a 1992 essay titled "The Dilemma of becoming an American:" Can I build two landscapes in one life? Can Lahore's Ravi ever flow into Washington's Potomac? For some immigrants, as I explained in my essay, the answer may be "yes."

We then moved on to a discussion about the intriguing ending of "The Reluctant Fundamentalist." One of the great merits of Hamid's novel, I told him, is the incredible quality of leaving space for the reader's thoughts to echo. What makes the ending both stunning and ambiguous is the seductive trap, which he skillfully laid all along and is based on the reader's own expectations and mindset. The novel thus becomes a mirror in which each reader sees his own image and prejudices. By drawing the reader into the monologue of Changez, the novel thus imparts urgency to the narrative, making it a highly entertaining work of fiction.

Having lived in the USA for thirty years what I believe will endure for first generation immigrants like Changez is the age-old question which I raised in a 1992 essay titled "The Dilemma of becoming an American:" Can I build two landscapes in one life? Can Lahore's Ravi ever flow into Washington's Potomac?

The print connection: Washington Book Festival (2003)

THE LIBRARY OF & LAURA CONGRESS BUSH

SATURDAY, OCTOBER 4, 2003, 10AM - 5PM
ON THE NATIONAL MALL, WASHINGTON, DC
W W W . L O C . G O V

The third National Book Festival arranged by the Library of Congress (LOC) and hosted by Laura Bush was held on The Mall in Washington D.C. on Saturday October 4, 2003. Unlike the usual antiquarian book fairs held in major American cities like New York, Los Angeles or Chicago, this one did not create a huge book store. The emphasis here was not on selling books by publishing houses but putting on display an abundance of themes and authors.

The distinctive feature of this book festival was a cornucopia of authors from diverse ethnicities and backgrounds. More than 80 award-winning authors appeared in eight separate tents or pavilions offering thousands of men, women and children — who turned up in spite of the threat of rain — a variety of choices. These tents were capable of accommodating an audience of two to three hundred people each and were boldly marked with what they offered with a huge sign on top: History and Biography, Fiction and Imagination, Storytelling, Poetry, Mystery and Thrillers, Home and Family and Teens and Children.

This annual event begun through the efforts of Laura Bush in 2001 — perhaps, the only constructive and humane act of the current administration — was supported by numerous sponsors like *The Washington Post* whose

Book World columnists and editors Jonathan Yardley, Michael Dirda and Marie Arana introduced authors to the audience and took a prominent role in publicizing the book festival. Other sponsors were the National Endowment of Arts which offers hundreds of thousands of dollars each year to talented and aspiring poets and novelists and several multinationals like AT&T.

> *James Billington, the librarian of Congress, talked of the 'centrality of books in Western civilization'. He explained how working with librarians in six overseas offices (Cairo, Jakarta, Islamabad, Nairobi, Delhi and Rio de Janeiro), area specialists from the Library of Congress acquire very important and valuable materials from more than 175 countries.*

Some 600 volunteers helped in organizing and managing the festival. Cable TV channel C-Span in its weekly program called "Book TV" carried six hours of live broadcast from the "History and Biography Pavilion". In a city that has been traumatized by unhappy events during the last few years, starting with 9/11 in 2001 and then the sniper attacks in 2002 in which 10 innocent human beings were fatally shot indiscriminately by two insane men, followed by Hurricane Isabel in September 2003, the bringing together of thousands of average Americans— people of all generations and backgrounds —in their common love and appreciation of books and authors was a welcome sight.

Speaking from the "Pavilion of History and Biography", James Billington, the librarian of Congress, put this succinctly when he talked of the 'centrality of books in Western civilization'. He explained how working with librarians in six overseas offices (Cairo, Jakarta, Islamabad, Nairobi, Delhi and Rio de Janeiro), area specialists from the Library of Congress acquire very important and valuable materials from more than 175 countries. This enables the various divisions at the LOC to provide reference service and access to reading materials and electronic resources about the cultures, history, economics, politics, religion, linguistics and literature of the world. As a result "this Library is everyman's passage to every country and region around the globe, with two thirds of its collection of books and periodicals written in more than 460 languages."

Among the prominent writers who appeared at the book festival was the actress Julie Andrews who is world famous for her performance in popular movies like "Mary Poppins" and "The Sound of Music". She is actually an author of several children's books under the name of Julie Andrews Edwards. Her most recent books are Dumpy and the Firefighters and Simeon's Gift both co-authored with her daughter. Julie Andrews' presence in the "Children's Pavilion" was a great attraction for the crowd of youngsters.

In the "Biography Pavilion" there were the ubiquitous Washington D.C. historians Michael Beschloss, James Brady and Robert Caro. Wherever you go, there they are! In much the same way, you had novelists Pat Conroy and Anita Shreve dominate the "Pavilion of the Novelists", although, thank God, the organizers did allow some fresh faces to appear this time. Prominent among these was Judith Cofer, a native of Puerto Rico who has been a recipient of several awards. Her recent novel *The Meaning of Consuelo* explores the dilemmas of national and ethnic identities in a multicultural America.

> *It is hoped that in keeping with the multicultural outlook of the Library of Congress future Washington Book Festivals will feature American writers from South Asia also, several of whom like Anita Desai, Bharati Mukherjee or Sara Suleri Goodyear are prominent in mainstream American literary circles.*

The "Storytelling Pavilion" was the most creative. It featured a host of storytellers from different cultures and ethnicities. There was Nancy Groce a specialist in urban folklore and American history. Ms Groce is a frequent commentator on Public Television and the BBC. She has written the *Encyclopedia of New York City* as well as *Songs of the City*. Then there were the Scottish-American Norman Kennedy, an internationally acclaimed folksinger and storyteller, Djimo Kouyate, a Senegalese-American musician and storyteller, who is a descendant of centuries-old West African tribe of "griots" (historian/storytellers) and Gayle Ross, a Native American from the Cherokee Nation of *"Trail of Tears"* fame. Her famous book is *The Legend of the Windigo: A Tale from Native North America* and a famous quote from there is: *Let those among us/ Who have left us to die /Know that we only slept /And now We live again.*

The "Poetry Pavilion" featured several American poets but the ones that impressed me most were the Indonesian-American, Li-Young Lee, and the former bohemian who lived in the Greek islands, David Mason. Lee fascinated the audience with his readings from his book of poems *The City in Which I love You.* His poems were not only evocative and mysterious but emphasized the immigrant sensibility. David Mason thrilled the audience by reading from his books *The Country I Remember* and *The Buried Houses.*

Finally, the "Home and Family Pavilion" featured the pragmatic nature of American life. Here the "How to" books prevailed. Secretary of State Colin Powell's wife touted a book about youth as America's Promise and in a bit of a bizarre presentation, Director of CIA, Tenet's wife promoted her book on how to repair household fixtures and appliances "when your husband is not there to help". I found this advice hilarious. How the wife of the most powerful spy in the world could not afford a plumber or a carpenter to do the job was nothing short of incredulous. As they say, only in America!

All in all the book festival was a resounding success except the conspicuous absence of any South-Asian-American authors. It is hoped that in keeping with the multicultural outlook of the Library of Congress future Washington Book Festivals will feature American writers from South Asia also, several of whom like Anita Desai, Bharati Mukherjee or Sara Suleri Goodyear are prominent in mainstream American literary circles.

Article 3

Celebrating Reading: Washington Book Festival (2004)

NEARLY 70,000 book lovers — at least one fourth of them children — gathered at the Mall in Washington DC on Saturday, October 9 to participate in the fourth annual National Book Festival, organized and sponsored by the Library of Congress and hosted by Laura Bush. The first lady, however, was not in attendance as she was campaigning for her husband in St Louis.

The 2004 festival featured more than 70 award-winning authors, illustrators and poets, including the alarmingly productive novelist Joyce Carol Oates, the prodigious author of 50 children's books, R.L. Stine, novelists Kate Lehrer and her broadcaster husband Jim Lehrer who mediated the first presidential debate, Ted Kooser who is the first poet laureate from a rural, mid-western state, my favourite poet Shirley Lim from California, Azar Nafisi, the celebrated Iranian author of *Reading Lolita in Teheran*, the Pulitzer prize winner Anna Quindlen of *The New York Times*, Cokie Roberts political analyst for ABC News and NPR, Kareem Abdul-Jabbar the famous basket-ball player turned author, Roland Mesnier, a former White House pastry chef now author of a bestseller cookbook, among many, many others.

A new pavilion, "Science Fiction & Fantasy", was added to this year's festival. The other pavilions, in addition to "Home & Family", were "Children", "Teens & Children", "Fiction & Imagination", "Mysteries & Thrillers", "History & Biography" and "Poetry".

Throughout the day authors discussed their work and what inspired them to write. Poets read their poems and novelists read excerpts from their work.

The devotees packed almost every author presentation, purchased books that were stacked up like firewood and then rushed to get the autographs.

The artist for this year's festival painting was award-winning illustrator Floyd Cooper. His whimsical image for the 2004 Festival is as imaginative as the act of reading. 25,000 posters featuring Cooper's painting were available free of charge during the festival and they were dutifully snapped up by the crowd.

This incredible enthusiasm behooves the Washington area. As Marie Arana, editor of *The Washington Post Book World* informed the audience, Washington DC is now the largest hard cover book market in the USA. The US market now publishes nearly 140,000 books every year. It is, therefore, ironic that in a city that celebrates reading so assiduously, if only a few senators had bothered to read the neo-con *Project for the New American Century* which recommended war with Iraq years before 9/11, may be mankind would have been spared the carnage in Iraq. We are told that the same members of Congress didn't read the *Patriotic Act* either before endorsing it into law.

As I sat there listening to writers and scholars, poets and journalists, I was struck by the great divide in America today. How come, given all this erudition, American voters at large appear to think that knowing something is elitist? So much so, that a knowledgeable Kerry or a brilliant Clinton has to dumb down his statements so that he does not offend the hillbillies.

One change that I saw in this book festival as compared to earlier ones, was a new propaganda strain introduced in the history and biography pavilion as well as pandering to authority by some authors in other pavilions. I hope this does not become a ticket to future appearances at this Festival. Carlos Eire, an ostensible religious scholar at Yale who fled from his homeland Cuba in 1962 when he was an 11-year-old boy, unleashed a tirade against Fidel Castro, ridiculing his father whom he called a thief. Although Marie Arana who introduced Carlos Eire's memoir *Waiting for Snow in Havana: Confessions of a Cuban Boy* paid glowing tributes to this work, what I heard was nothing sublime. According to Mr Eire, "Castro is the worst dictator the world has ever seen. He killed more people than Pinochet."

And then there was Azar Nafisi, the now celebrated author of *Reading Lolita in Teheran: A Memoir in Books*. Although her book is interesting and tows the familiar American official criticism of the rulers of Iran, her presentation at the biography pavilion bordered on the commonplace and the silly. Finally, there was Cokie Roberts who praised Laura Bush to be one of the so-called "Founding Mothers" which is the title of her book. Need I say more?

The authors I truly enjoyed at this festival were: Joyce Carol Oates, Jim and wife Kate Lehrer and the poetess Shirley Lim. Author of 70 books, Joyce Carol Oates' new hypnotic novel *The Falls* juxtaposes nature's majesty which in this case is the Niagara Falls with a man-made monstrosity of nuclear and toxic waste known as Love Canal. This backdrop underlines a family saga of self-destruction and redemption in the 1950's. Widowed on her wedding night when her new husband, a young minister and latent homosexual, throws himself into the falls, Ariah Littrell, the plain, awkward daughter of a minister, henceforth considers herself damned. The novel thus becomes a creative dialogue with the roiling cauldron of contemporary American culture.

The broadcaster Jim Lehrer gave a highly entertaining speech promoting his new 14th novel *Flying Crows* which is based in the Midwest. The opening reminded me of one V.S. Naipaul's famous novels *A House for Mr Biswas*. Kate Lehrer explained that her novel *Confessions of a Bigamist* was not autobiographical. While the crowd roared with laughter, she explained that she did not need two husbands because she is already married to Jim who —with all his various 24/7 activities — is like being married to seven husbands already.

> *The authors I truly enjoyed at this festival were: Joyce Carol Oates, Jim and wife Kate Lehrer and the poetess Shirley Lim... With tenderness, precision and verve Lim sings a rich song of exile. Her lines speak of loss — of family, country, self- -yet what is lost is also what is found.*

Before I conclude with a poem by Shirley Lim, I want to say a brief word on how wonderful an institution the Library of Congress is. It is both a national library and an architectural marvel to behold. For many a day for the last 26 years I have sat in the Jefferson Main Reading Room with its ornate window arches and its copper dome and enjoyed reading a wealth of books. For those of us who are familiar with Paris, it reminds one of *Palais Garnier* with its Beaux-Arts style.

James Billington, a Rhodes Scholar and a former Professor of history at Harvard and Princeton has been the Librarian of Congress since 1987. It was under his leadership that in 2000, the Library of Congress National Book Festival was created. Also under his guidance the NDL (National Digital Library) program has come into being. This incredible program now makes 24 million historical items and publications available freely on-line.

Finally, my favourite poet Shirley Lim who like me immigrated to the United States some 25 years ago from Asia. She is currently professor of English at the University of California at Santa Barbara. With tenderness, precision and verve Lim sings a rich song of exile. Her lines speak of loss — of family, country, self--yet what is lost is also what is found.

In a moving poem titled "Learning to love America" she writes:

because I walk barefoot in my house
because I have nursed my son at my breast
because he is a strong American boy
because I have seen his eyes redden when he is asked who he is
because he answers I don't know
because to have a son is to have a country
because my son will bury me here
because countries are in our blood and we bleed them
because it is late and too late to change my mind
because it is time.

Article 4

Three Comments from DAWN B&A

Summer Reading Agenda: (*Dawn*, June 10, 2007.)

Javed Amir is the author of Writing *Across Boundaries* and *Modern Soap*

I had *read* James Joyce's *Ulysses* some 40 years ago but a new world opened this past spring when I *studied* it again for over 16 hours with Darmouth professor James Hefferman who has spent his life teaching Joyce.

According to him, you cannot read Ulysses. You can only *re-read* it.

I would venture to add not only re-read but *listen* also as I plan to do this summer to the Irish production by Naxos. Directed by Roger Marsh, the novel is narrated by Marcella Riordan as Molly and Jim Norton as everyone else. Both readers are Dubliners who have absorbed the novel into their beings. The 38 hours rendering comes in 22 CDs and I am told captures the accents, cadences and intonations of Joyce's masterpiece.

My second summer reading is Michael Ondaatje's new novel *Divisadero*. I am told Ondaatje does not write his novels with a pre-existing outline. He is a great improviser. Like Garcia Márquez, he stops writing the moment he knows what is next. Ondaatje begins with fragmentary images or situations and starts constructing his novel from those fragments. The man really has an unbelievable imagination and his novel echoes Nietzche's immortal remark, "We have art so that we shall not be destroyed."

Finally I am going to read a little book of essays that I picked up in March this year while traveling in New Mexico. The book, published in 1973, contains essays by D.H. Lawrence and Carl Jung. Edited by Tony Hillerman, the book is titled *The Spell of New Mexico*.

Needless to say, my summer readings will continue after I finish reading these books. Such are the rigors of retirement.

II

Author's Favorites:

According to Darmouth professor James Hefferman, who has spent his life teaching Joyce, you cannot read Ulysses. You can only re-read it.

*Many of our writers and poets have graced the pages of **Books & Authors** by writing for us. The presence of others has been registered through their books that we have excerpted or reviewed. To have their participation on this occasion we sent at random the following question to a number of them: "Which character/ personality in a book you have read has fascinated you most and why?" Here are the answers we received from those who were kind enough to reply to our query* ---**Books & Authors Editor. (April 2005)**

Javed Amir is the author of Writing *Across Boundaries* and *Modern Soap*

I have enjoyed writing books. But looking back I wish I would have been a maker of films also. Why? Because, words are weak. They do not always do what we expect them to. Less ambiguous, perhaps, is the communication through a camera. Hence the cliche, a picture is worth a thousand words. My favourite creative personality, therefore, who also is a writer of books like *In Search of Mystery* is Bernardo Bertolucci, the world renowned Italian film director. His movies are expressionistic, meaning that they transgress the realities of everyday life and using several visual techniques aim for the mood and aura of the surrealistic. His controversial 1972 film "Last Tango in Paris" is a romantic and sensuous work of art. It is the story of a middle aged man who is torn by despair at the suicide of his wife and embarks on a purely sexual sadomasochistic affair with a young girl, who in the end, kills him. As the dying protagonist staggers onto the balcony of the apartment and gazes longingly for the last time at life and the Parisian rooftops drenched in a golden twilight, only Mirza Ghalib's words could match this aesthetic visual drama:

Go Hath Mein Jumbish Nahin, Aankhon Mein To Dum Hai
Rahne Do Abhi Sagar-O-Meena Mere Aage

(Though the hands don't move, the eyes are alive
Wine and goblet, let them stay in front of me.)

Mohsin Hamid is the author of *Moth Smoke* and has been *"attempting to become the author of a second novel for the past five years"*

At the moment, I must say I am deeply fascinated by the character of Jean-Baptiste Clamence, the narrator-protagonist of *The Fall* by Albert Camus. We — the readers — encounter him in a bar in Amsterdam and he proceeds to tell us a brilliant confession which implicates not only him, but also leftist-intellectual Paris, and even his reader. His voice — conversational, charming, intelligent — is one of the great achievements of 20th century literature, and he has taught me a great deal.

Zulfikar Ghose is the author of *The Murder of Aziz Khan and Selected Poems*

> *As the dying protagonist staggers onto the balcony of the apartment in Bertolucci's film, he gazes longingly for the last time at life and the Parisian rooftops drenched in a golden twilight. Only Mirza Ghalib's words could match this aesthetic visual drama:*
>
> *Jo haath mai junbish nahin ankhon mai to dum hai Rehnay do abhee saghar o meena merey agai.*

Not one but a host of characters keep me entertained every day, and I spend more time with them than with real people. Hamlet is constantly sulking in a corner of my room where, candle in hand and her eyes glazed, Lady Macbeth sometimes comes walking past pursued by Falstaff's laughter; I look out of the window and there's Heathcliff and Catherine running past hand in hand; you've only got to say 'Dickens' and an army of characters goes marching across my eyes; then there's Diderot's Jacques and a whole family of friends in Balzac. I'm reminded of one of those Soviet style May Day parades which went on and on, so endless are the characters who continue to fascinate me. But if I must give you one, it has to be a composite of Murphy, Watt, Molloy and Malone in Beckett's novels who combine in my mind as The Unnamable whose being fills me with wonder, astonishment, joy and horror all at once. The Unnamable is all of us, all humanity compressed into one abstract being, the living and the dead caught in a timeless presence in a meaningless universe.

Muneeza Shamsie is the editor of *A Dragonfly in The Sun: An Anthology of Pakistani Writing in English*

> *On several occasions, I have talked to senior diplomats of both Pakistan and India in Washington. I must confess I have found only rigid mindsets. These officials cling to a destructive past and seem bogged down in a bureaucratic quagmire demanding a "full resolution of disputes".*

Edward James has been an enigma and mystery to me always. He was an eccentric American millionaire, who lived in Mexico, owned many spectacular paintings by Dali, Magritte and Picasso and was said to be the illegitimate son of Edward VII. His Sussex home, West Dean, had been converted into our school.

I was riveted by his 1982 memoir Swans Reflecting Elephants: My Early Years edited by George Melly, based on taped interviews, which told of a sad lonely life interwoven with wonderful salacious gems about the rich and famous. He claimed his mother was the illegitimate daughter of Edward VII, Henry James a cousin, and the James' wealth was 'Old' (American timber and railways), but his father died when he was five. His mother and sisters terrorized him, prep school was a trauma, Eton a disaster, Oxford a misery; his marriage to ballerina Tilly Losch, a long heartache.

In 1991 Edward James: A Surrealist Life by John Lowe challenged "Melly's book" and stated James had wept with anger when he saw it. The bizarre James had fed Melly "fabrications" which Melly believed. Lowe drew on archives to assert there was no royal blood, no connection to Henry James, no predatory female monsters whether mother, sisters or wife, no 'old American' money, but yes, undoubted wealth, great unhappiness and a love of nature and art, which led to the creation of famous architectural follies in the Mexican jungle. Nevertheless, Lowe's book is very boring, while Melly's attained a mesmerizing, memorable, psychological truth. Therein lies the nature of art and storytelling

Bapsi Sidhwa is author of *Ice-Candy-Man and An American Brat*

Anna, in Tolstoy's wonderful novel, Anna Karinina, is one of my favourite fictional characters. I love her for her beauty, her sophistication and the passion that slowly consumes her and brings us face to face with the vulnerability all of us as women share and can empathize with. Tolstoy has an uncanny insight into the nature of women and in creating her character with compassion has given us an unforgettable and vivid portrait of a complex woman trapped in the mores of her time.

III

COMMENT : "Should India and Pakistan Bury the Hatchet"

(Dawn, 2003.)

Javed Amir writes:

Should Pakistan and India bury the hatchet is hardly the question. The real question is how to bring this irrational historic animosity on the tormented and nuclear-armed subcontinent to an end.

On several occasions, I have talked to senior diplomats of both Pakistan and India in Washington. I must confess I have found only rigid mindsets. These officials cling to a destructive past and seem bogged down in a bureaucratic quagmire demanding a "full resolution of disputes".

What leaders of the two countries desperately need is the realization that this is not a zero sum game. They must urgently engage in result-oriented dialogue and look for new, win-win solutions.

In this regard, it is critical that they grasp the reality that deep-rooted disputes cannot be ever "fully resolved". You can only transform them. And how do you do that? With the explosive rise of fundamentalism and hate in both countries, rational leaders on both sides should begin serious discussions not only on confidence building measures like movement of people, ideas and trade but jump start a broad based people movement where scholars, journalists, farmers, students, artists, businessmen and politicians on either side try to win the hearts and minds of each other's nation.

Article 5

Tariq Ali Speaks of Peace

Tariq Ali spoke at Johns Hopkins University, Baltimore. (Dawn, November 2003)

An audience of about 200 attended the book's launching at the Johns Hopkins University in Baltimore in late October. I had not seen Tariq for many years now. Like all of us of his generation, he has a lot of grey hair and there he was in his telegenic red shirt talking down the Bush administration. His unforgiving indictment of the "American Empire" was vintage Tariq Ali and brought back memories of 1960's Lahore when as a Ravian he courageously led the protest against Ayub's tyrannical governor Kalabagh.

Son of the illustrious journalist and editor, Mazhar Ali Khan, Tariq chose socialism as his creed and went on to study in Oxford and made London his new home. Ruby Lal, assisstant professor of Anthroplogy at Johns Hopkins, introduced him as one who debated Kissinger and effectively protested against the Vietnam war. She recounted the dozen books he has written on world history and politics, including the bestseller *Clash of Fundamentalisms*. As a man who appears in many garbs, she said, he is also working on an opera on Ayatollah Khomeini.

Tariq began his lecture — which was covered by CSPAN cable TV — by stating that when the events of 9/11 took place there were two possible solutions. One military and the other political. He said that he argued with several Bush people that if the United States invaded Afghanistan and occupied it, not only would terrorism increase in the world, but that they would fail to dismantle a global organization like Al Qaeda.

On the other hand, if two key political problems were resolved it would make the world a safer place. One, a serious attempt at solving the Palestinian-Israeli conflict and the other, the lifting of sanctions against Iraq which had led to the deaths of half a million Iraqi children. If these two problems were resolved, Tariq said, it would have stopped the flow of young, educated Arabs to organizations like Al Qaeda. Instead, the Bush administration decided to do the exact opposite. Not only did they attack Afghanistan and occupy it, they went ahead in their unilateral invasion of Iraq on the basis of lies and deceptions.

Tariq emphasized that in his book *Bush in Babylon: The Recolonization of Iraq* he points out twenty different occasions on which President Bush repeated his claim that Iraq possessed weapons of mass destruction. Tony Blair, whom he called Bush's "fellow conspirator" claimed that Saddam could launch WMD's that could reach London in 45 minutes. These, said Tariq, were total and complete lies.

> *According to Tariq, the principal reason to attack Iraq was a demonstration of American military power, not simply to the Arab world, but to the world at large especially to future capitalist economic rivals in Europe and the Far East like China.*

He added that in Febraury 2003, eight million people protested globally against the war in Iraq before the actual war started. This, he said was unprecedented. Not that a massive radicalization was taking place of the people but that they were getting increasingly nervous of a superpower out of control, the only single empire in the world which believed that it could dominate the world at will.

Turning to the analysis of the real reasons for going to war against Iraq, Tariq pointed out that it was precisely because Iraq did not possess any WMDs that the Bush administration decided to invade Iraq. Had they possessed any such lethal weapons, the American Empire would have never waged a war on Iraq. Nor was the Saddam-Al Qaeda connection worthy of any credibility. Nor, said Tariq, was oil the principal reason for this invasion. There are many other ways to get oil from Iraq, he said, including decoy companies that were buying Iraqi oil for America in spite of the so-called sanctions.

According to Tariq, the principal reason to attack Iraq was a demonstration of American military power, not simply to the Arab world, but to the world at large especially to future capitalist economic rivals in Europe and the Far East like China. He compared this demonstration of imperial power to the launching of atomic bombs on Japan at the end of the Second World War, when the latter had already been militarily defeated and the only reason for Hiroshima and Nagasaki was to tell the Soviet Union and emerging Communist China *"This is what we are capable of."*

Turning to the growing resistance in Iraq, Tariq mentioned that there are over 40 different resistance organizations, large and small. He expressed sorrow for the American soldiers who were sent to die in Iraq. The key fact of the resistance, said Tariq, is that it is decentralized — the classic first stage guerrilla warfare against an occupying army. Whether these groups will move to the second stage and establish an Iraq National Liberation Front remains to be seen.

He rebutted the argument that if America leaves Iraq now it would be a disaster. *"Excuse me,"* he remarked, *"It is a disaster, because you are there."* Withdrawing from Iraq, on the contrary, would enable the Iraqi people to exercise their national right of self determination, he said. He reminded the audience, that many bad things had happened in the US recently, but it is not a fascist state as some exaggerate it to be. The Bush administration used 9/11 to suppress the Americans. But that stage was over. *"Now you can speak up."* Since the Democratic Party is pathetic as an opposition, the people of America have to wage this struggle to end American imperialism in the world and prevent more "blowbacks" in the future.

> *I wonder if the deeply divided and inept Bush administration has the ability to think strategically. Time and again, in the last three years we have seen their ignorance of elementary governance matched only by their greed. When the US administration fails even to get support from Canada and Mexico, it is difficult to dignify it with long term strategic vision.*

After speaking for about an hour, Tariq invited the audience to ask questions. He was asked what was the state of the anti-war movement in Britain? He replied that it had suffered a huge demoralization when it failed to stop the war. However, with the growing resistance in Iraq, the movement had received a "second spurt". Since the British government had failed to guarantee President Bush's security in a forthcoming visit, many outdoor activities had been canceled and it would now only be a "helicopter visit."

To the question whether the Iraq war was a first step towards a greater Israel he said that was only a small element and repeated in detail his theory of the demonstration of imperial power. Someone then asked that after the "military victory" in Iraq was not America's worst fear that a democratic Iraq would be a Shiite Islamic state? Tariq tackled that question masterfully by going into history and showing how no oil producing nation was ever been allowed by the Americans to have a true democracy. If democracy is allowed at all, he said, it will be a controlled one where the interests of the empire would dominate.

Finally, came the question, "Since Saddam was a brutal tyrant was not his removal at some level a good thing?" To that Tariq reminded the audience that only the people of Iraq had the right to remove their leader. Secondly, by removing him America had only increased the tyranny, bloodshed and suffering of the Iraqi people which was worse than when Saddam was in power.

Although I thoroughly enjoyed Tariq Ali's presentation, I have some reservations about his main theory on why America attacked Iraq. That imperial powers demonstrate their military domination when they feel that they might be economically in relative decline has some historical merit. But I wonder if the deeply divided and inept Bush administration has the ability to think strategically. Time and again, in the last three years we have seen their ignorance of elementary governance matched only by their greed. When the US administration fails even to get support from Canada and Mexico, it is difficult to dignify it with long term strategic vision.

Finally, in keeping with the Bush administration's forte in tactical victories at the expense of strategic thinking, the Iraq War has provided a colossal diversion. It has wiped out the truly damaging domestic news of the looting of the small investors in the USA by colleagues and supporters of the Bush administration, namely the corrupt villains who ran Enron, Global Crossing, Wcom, Tyco, the mutual fund industry to mention a few. We are talking billions of dollars of financial crimes here! That politically damaging news in which millions of Americans lost their life savings, is no longer front-page news thanks to the war in Iraq.

A Failed State with Nuclear Weapons

By Javed Amir

From the February 2003 issue of *World Press Review* (VOL. 50, No. 2)

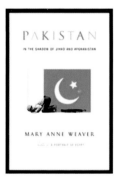

It was June 1989. Until then Benazir Bhutto had enjoyed enormous popularity in Washington. Then, according to a senior State Department official, attitudes began to change. When she stood on the floor of the U.S. Congress, promising, to thunderous applause, that Pakistan neither possessed nor intended to assemble a nuclear bomb—the very day after she had received a detailed briefing on Pakistan's weapons program from the director of the CIA—Bhutto's worth was diminished in the eyes of the United States. In less than a year she ceased to be prime minister.

Mary Anne Weaver's book *Pakistan: In the Shadow of Jihad and Afghanistan* (Farrar, Straus & Giroux) is full of such anecdotes, which vividly portray personalities and pivotal moments of Pakistan's recent turbulent history. Although several sections of her book have already appeared in *The New Yorker*, where Weaver is a correspondent, most of her material has an engaging quality to it. The exception is later chapters, which tend to be repetitive and confuse events in the 1980s with the present. Instead of abstract political analysis this book actually brings to life the various regions and landscapes of Pakistan, the interplay of Pakistani politics and society, and above all, its surreal leaders of the last two decades, namely Zia-ul-Haq, Benazir Bhutto, Nawaz Sharif, and Pervez Musharraf.

"A bearer wearing a golden turban with green cockscombs entered the drawing room with coffee and tea," she writes, "as I asked Gen. Musharraf how he would compare himself to Gen. Zia-ul-Haq. He smiled. 'The biggest difference is that Zia wanted to be there forever. He was also much more religious than I am. He used religion to ensure his own power, and I strongly believe that religion should not be manipulated for political gains.

Also, the people of Pakistan, perhaps, were not really with Zia, but they certainly are supportive of my government and me.'

In a devastating comparison, Weaver shows Musharraf and Zia as chips off the same block. Both products of British India, both military rulers who suspended the constitution and banned political activity, and whose armies remained their primary constituencies, both holding fraudulent referendums to legitimize their usurpation of power, both shunned by the West and then, as the phoenix rose from the ashes, both reborn: now, Musharraf; then, Zia, thanks to Washington's Afghan wars.

> *Weaver shows Musharraf and Zia as chips off the same block. Both products of British India, both military rulers who suspended the constitution, both shunned by the West and reborn thanks to Washington's Afghan wars.*

Repeatedly in the book, Weaver asks the question: Who was Zia and who is Musharraf? Zia, she says, was wily and adroit, a master manipulator of power who could be disarmingly candid at times. "I've discovered," he told her in 1982, "that gaining power is much easier than giving it up." On the other hand, Musharraf is often described as a "soldier's soldier" and he likes to be seen as a genuine patriot in the mold of Ataturk. But is he? According to Weaver, Musharraf is a difficult man to describe, for each time she saw him he looked astonishingly different, depending upon whom he was seeing, where he was, and the mood in which he had dressed that day. A former commanding officer remarked, "He's a cipher who can be anything."

At the end of the book, Weaver describes an elegant dinner party in which a female guest asked Musharraf what he was doing about lawlessness in Karachi. With a flourish Musharraf reached into his breast pocket, pulled a silver-plated pistol and remarked: "This is how I protect myself."

Continuing her portrait of Pakistan as a failed state with nuclear weapons, Weaver exposes the bald ambitions of both Nawaz Sharif and Benazir Bhutto. The former for engineering the bizarre incident of PK-805, in which he tried to kill Musharraf, and the latter for being a slave of her feudal heritage, which catered to her illusion that it was her birthright to rule.

In this book she candidly criticizes U.S. policy, which abandoned Pakistan and Afghanistan to the ravages of a drug and arms culture after the Soviet withdrawal in 1989. In addition, two decades later President Ronald

Reagan's Afghan freedom fighters turned into Frankenstein's monsters determined to attack America and launch a worldwide jihad.

Although Weaver portrays a frightening picture of Pakistan, she fails to dig deeper. Instead she merely entertains, like the American ambassador who remarked that "Islamabad is like a New York cemetery: half the size, but twice as dead." Ostensibly this book is also about jihad. The motivations of militant Islam and its raison d'être are simply glossed over.

Unlike two other recent books on Pakistan—*The United States and Pakistan* by the diplomat Dennis Kux and *Pakistan: Eye of the Storm* by the British journalist Owen Bennett Jones—Weaver's work lacks analytical probing. In her worldview, for example, jihad would appear only to be about beards and burqahs. Nowhere does she explain in a meaningful way that it is also a reaction to poverty, imperialism, and indignity.

> *Although Weaver portrays a frightening picture of Pakistan, she fails to dig deeper. In her worldview, for example, jihad would appear only to be about beards and burqahs.*

Article 7

An Early Warning

PAGE G2 / THURSDAY, MAY 14, 1992   The Washington Times

Islam is not a menace to the West

Let me respond to Amos Perlmutter's May 10 Commentary section article on Afghanistan.

I'm amazed by the art of myth-making. According to Mr. Perlmutter, "Islamic fundamentalism represents the most potentially destabilizing force," a force that is a "dangerous threat" to the "post-Cold War international order." It kind of reminds me of the dangerous threat the Sandinistas once posed to Harlingen, Texas.

I guess now that Afghanistan has fallen to the "Islamic fundamentalists," we have no choice but to resurrect our old friend the "domino theory" and see the monolithic "green peril" sweep from South Asia to North Africa to Central Asia.

No doubt Afghanistan is in a big mess today but it has been that way with or without "Islamic fundamentalism."

Ostensibly, Central Asia is united by a common Islamic religion, but it is also deeply divided by complex ethnic rivalries, varied cultural leanings and different economic needs.

Out of the 60 million people who inhabit Central Asia, 50 million are Sunni Muslims and fewer than 10 million are hostile Shi'ites. Two states, Armenia and Georgia, are Christian. The recent mosque-building fervor in some states is an understandable rediscovery of a people cut off from their culture for 70 years more than anything else.

It is startling to note that 41 percent of Kazakhstan's population is Russian and only 40 percent are Kazakhs. Scores of Uz-

The Sacred Mosque at Mecca
– National Geographic Society

beks, Ukrainians and Tartars constitute the rest. It is unlikely, therefore, that Islam or fundamentalism is going to be an overriding factor in the future course of Central Asia. The crucial destabilizing element both in Central Asia and Afghanistan instead is the jagged mosaic of multiethnic states.

Mr. Perlmutter's point that the mujahdeen's victory in Afghanistan will end up fueling fundamentalist Muslim forces in India resulting in "Islamic terror" is greatly exaggerated. The danger to secular India is not from the minority religion of Islam but from the tyranny of the majority religion of Hinduism.

It is mind-boggling that we always hear of "Islamic fundamentalism" but never of "Hindu fundamentalism," as personified by the militant and extremist Bharatiya Janata Party, which is one of the ruling factions in India. Furthermore, Indian Muslims do not share any common cultural history or empathy with the Afghans, who are regarded as backward, tribal people who also happen to be Muslims.

Finally, when are some Western scholars going to understand that there is more to Islam than fundamentalism?

It is in our enlightened mutual interest not to create a bogeyman out of "Islamic fundamentalism," which is at best an oxymoron.

The concepts of "Ijtihad" (exercise of judgment) and "Ijma" (concensus) in Islam clearly call for updating and reconciling Islamic societies to present-day needs. No doubt there are some extremists in Islamic countries as there are anywhere else. However, there is a vast majority of Western-educated Muslims living in countries from Morocco to Pakistan who clearly desire a reconciliation between Islam and Western social and political thought. This Muslim majority does not look upon the Western world as its enemy.

It is time we in the West try to encourage their efforts to separate religion and politics in Islam rather than indulging in mindless propaganda.

JAVED AMIR
Beltsville

As I read *The Washington Post* on July 27, 2013, I am once again struck by the madness of US foreign policy during the disastrous Bush and to a lesser extent in the Obama eras. What is truly shocking is how time and time again, the American people are duped into wars that were totally un-necessary. Imagine Iraq and Afghanistan wars had 90% approval rating of the public at one time. Here is an excerpt from *The Post*:

US SUPPORT FOR AFGHAN WAR PLUNGES TO NEW LOW.

Only 28% of Americans say the <u>war in Afghanistan</u> has been worth fighting for…the drop in approval was matched by an 11% increase, to 67%, in those who say the war has not been worth fighting…Support for the war was extraordinarily high at the inception, with more than 90% saying that they supported the US-led effort through early 2002…Eventually American soldiers reached about 100,000 in 2010 precisely the time support for the war began to slide precipitously—a year marked by highest number of US military deaths. By July 2010 total US casualties in the war reached 2,248 dead and more than 19,000 wounded, according to Pentagon figures…Today, Obama administration officials did not dispute recent news reports that complete withdrawal, or "zero option" was on the table.

It may be recalled, that public support similarly sank for <u>the Iraq</u> war to its lowest point

--33%--in November 2011, just a month before the final US troop withdrawal.

According to conventional wisdom the Afghanistan and Iraq Wars of the 21st century would never have happened if America had not been attacked on Sept 11, 2001. The real question is: was 9/11 a confirmation of the views of the right in the USA or a God-send pretext for wars of choice which, as my piece below clearly reveals, had been preached years before 9/11 took place? Further, as argued by some authors like George Soros or Tariq Ali whose books I have reviewed in the Book Reviews section, even after the horrific event of 9/11, neither Iraq nor Afghanistan were wars of necessity.

More than 20 years ago, here is what I wrote in an op-ed in *The Washington Times*. I leave it to the reader to draw his own conclusions from the questions posed above.

ISLAM IS NOT A MENACE TO THE WEST

The Washington Times, **May 14, 1992.**

> *What is truly shocking is how time and time again, the American people are duped into wars that were totally unnecessary.*

I am amazed by the art of mythmaking by Amos Perlmutter of The Heritage Foundation in his commentary on Afghanistan. According to him, "Islamic Fundamentalism poses a dangerous threat to the post-Cold War international order." No doubt Afghanistan is in a big mess today but it has been that way with or without "Islamic Fundamentalism".

Ostensibly, Central Asia is united by a common Islamic religion, but it is also deeply divided by complex ethnic rivalries, varied cultural leanings and different economic needs.

Out of the 60 million people who inhabit Central Asia, 50 million are Sunni Muslims and fewer than 10 million are hostile Shi'ites. Two states, Armenia and Georgia, are Christian. The recent mosque building fervor in some states is an understandable rediscovery of a people cut off from their culture for 70 years of USSR occupation, more than anything else.

It is an eye-opener to note that 41% of Kazakhstan's population is Russian and only 40% are Kazakhs. Scores of Uzbeks, Ukrainians and Tartars constitute the rest. It is unlikely, therefore, that Islam or fundamentalism is going to be an over-riding factor in the future course of Central Asia. The crucial destabilizing element both in Central Asia and Afghanistan instead is the jagged mosaic of multiethnic states.

Mr Perlmutter's alarmist point that the Mujahideen's victory in Afghanistan will end up fueling fundamentalist Muslim forces in India resulting in "Islamic terror" is greatly exaggerated. The danger to secular India is not from the minority religion of Islam but from the tyranny of the majority religion of Hinduism.

It is mind-boggling that we always hear of "Islamic Fundamentalism" but never of "Hindu Fundamentalism" as personified by the militant and extremist BJP, which is one of the ruling factions in India. Furthermore, Indian Muslims do not share any common cultural history or empathy with the Afghans, who are regarded as backward, tribal people who also happen to be Muslims.

It is unfortunate that some Western scholars fail to understand that there is more to Islam than fundamentalism. Or is it a deliberate distortion to create a bogeyman in some vested interest's search for the "green peril" to replace the demise of the "red peril?" Please note that at best "Islamic fundamentalism" is an oxymoron.

The concepts of "Ijtihad" (exercise of judgment) and "Ijma" (consensus) in Islam clearly call for updating and reconciling Islamic societies to present-day needs. No doubt there are some extremists in Islamic countries as there are anywhere else. However, there is a vast majority of Western-educated Muslims living in countries from Morocco to Pakistan who clearly desire reconciliation between Islam and western social and political thought. This Muslim majority does not look upon the Western world as its enemy.

It is time we in the West try to encourage their efforts to separate religion and politics in Islam rather than indulging in mindless propaganda.

It is unfortunate that some Western scholars fail to understand that there is more to Islam than fundamentalism. Or is it a deliberate distortion to create a bogeyman in some vested interest's search for the "green peril" to replace the demise of the "red peril?"

Book Review 1

Scheherazade Goes West

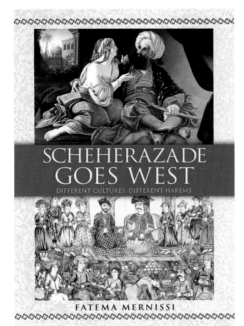

Scheherazade Goes West: different cultures, different harems is a fascinating book by an Arab feminist from Morocco. Fatema Mernissi is a professor of sociology at the University of Rabat and is widely considered one of the greatest living scholars of the Quran. She has been a visiting lecturer at Harvard and Berkeley. Her recent books are the *Veil and the Male elite; Dreams of Trespass: Tales of Harem Girlhood and Beyond the Veil*.

In Scheherazade Goes West she offers a provocative look at the differences between Arab and Western views of sex, eroticism, relationships and love. In the process, she challenges the Western assumption that women have it much better in the West than almost everywhere else. In 1994 when she went to promote her book *Dreams of Trespass*, she was perplexed when Western audiences reacted to the word harem as though she had uttered something obscene. Actually the opening sentence of the book is *"I was born in a harem."*

Eager to understand this phenomenon, she began to study European and American art, dance and literature. She discovered that whereas in Islamic miniatures and literature, Muslim men represent harem women as active participants who ride horses or are uncontrollable sexual partners, Western artists such as Matisse, Ingres and Picasso show them as nude and passive creatures where omnipotent men reign supreme over obedient, brain-dead women.

Such perceptions, says Mernissi, are yet another example of the cultural misconceptions forming the great divide between the East and the West. To the Easterner, a harem means a private space but is also synonymous with a literal and figurative prison. In other words, harem is a state of mind when someone dictates to you how you should be.

In a brilliant chapter, "Mind as Erotic Weapon" Mernissi explains the true significance of the often misunderstood tale of Scheherazade in the West. *The Thousand and One Nights* also known in the West as *The Arabian Nights* is a tragedy that begins with king Shaharyar's betrayal by his wife resulting in his violent revenge where he slaughters hundreds of virgins after marrying them for one night. However, the story ends as a fairy tale owing to Scheherazade's intellectual capacity to read her husband's mind.

> *Whereas in Islamic miniatures and literature, Muslim men represent harem women as active participants who ride horses or are uncontrollable sexual partners, Western artists such as Matisse, Ingres and Picasso show them as nude and passive creatures where omnipotent men reign supreme.*

There is a political dimension to *The Thousand and One Nights*. The king was not looking for sex. He was looking for a psychotherapist, says Mernissi. Westerners who have misread this story fail to realize that this is a political story. Scheherazade not only saved herself but the entire kingdom by slowly changing the mind of the chief decision-maker, the king. Here was a woman who through dialogue and not through the use of violent armies transformed a cruel despot to a civilized human being.

Furthermore, says Mernissi, there is a great feminist message in this story. The problem she says is that men are not capable of handling fear. They immediately resort to violence. Women, on the other hand, are natural dialogue-builders. Thus there is an inherent symbolism in the tale of Scheherazade. It links humanism with feminism. And, if we look further, the bond between political pluralism and feminism in today's troubled Islamic societies was foreshadowed by the Scheherazade-Shaharyar tale.

Anyway, why did the enlightened West, obsessed with democracy and human rights, discard Scheherazade's brainy sensuality and political message in their interpretation of the tale? Both the 1704 translation into French by Galland and the twentieth century ballets of Nijinsky used her body as the sole source of sexual pleasure. Then there was Edgar Allen Poe, who killed off Scheherazade and claimed that she enjoyed her own murder, in his story *"The Thousand-and-Second Tale of Scheharazade."*

According to Mernissi the West's understanding of this famous tale and the harem world is skin deep, cosmetic and superficial. *"The storytellers yearning for a dialogue between man and woman found no echo in the West."* Why was that? Because Western men do not want to lose ground to their own women. Imagine what Kant, the great German philosopher, said when he mused that a woman's beauty was to be found in her silence.

In her chapter entitled "Intelligence versus Beauty," Mernissi explains Western male fantasies of the harem by saying that "Could it be that Ingres' odalisques were a kind of a shield to protect him from his own emotions?" In other words, Kant's ideal of a brainless beauty, the power of painted images like Ingres' "Turkish Bath" and Hollywood movies like Elvis Pressley's "Harum Scarum" point to three major weapons or "images" used by men in the West to dominate their women.

The reason, she says that Matisse was not interested in painting a dynamic and brainy Mughal queen like Nur Jahan, skillfully hunting tigers, or Kamal Ataturk's ideal of beauty in Turkish women throwing away their veil and flying planes, was that the Western men did not want to stop oppressing women.

> *"The Taliban," says Mernissi, "is the Muslim version of the Salem witch trials." Muslims are not stuck in the Stone Age. They too are concerned with modernity and reform. From burqa to miniskirt, she emphasizes, it is the same form of male oppression against women worldwide. Different cultures, different harems.*

Mernissi has spent much of her life trying to cross boundaries, seeking solidarity among women in finding common ground. Recently with the Islamic diaspora, she finds it her mission to rehabilitate the image of the Muslim world, particularly that of the Muslim women. She quotes Naomi Wolf author of the Beauty Myth who states: *"A Western cultural fixation on female thinness is not an obsession about female beauty, it is an obsession about female obedience."*

Although it is difficult to classify *Scheherazade Goes West* which at times is scholarly and at times playful, Mernissi's message is clear. She wants the West to understand that Muslim women are diverse with different views on the role of religion in their lives. *"The Taliban," she says, "is the*

Muslim version of the Salem witch trials." Muslims are not stuck in the Stone Age. They too are concerned with modernity and reform. From burqa to miniskirt, she emphasizes, it is the same form of male oppression against women worldwide. Different cultures, different harems. (June 2002).

Scheherazade Goes West By Fatema Mernissi, Washington Square Press ISBN: 0-7434-1243-5 228 pages. $14.00

Bridging Two Worlds

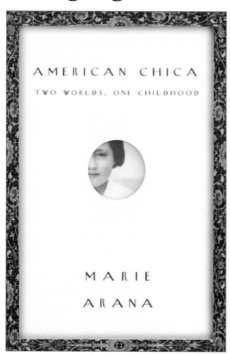

The universal question for the twenty-first century, Carlos Fuentes writes, is how do we deal with the Other? In the last two decades some 15 million new immigrants — predominantly from Latin America and Asia — have migrated to the United States. This fourth wave of immigration in American history has resulted in what has been termed by some as the "browning of America".

The Washington Posts Book World's Editor, Marie Arana's memoir *American Chica: Two Worlds, one Childhood* captures this changing cadence and color of modern America in all its positive manifestations, with deep and intimate understanding. Millions of young new immigrant women will relate to *American Chica*, who is neither *gringa* nor *latina* but a whole new person who lives on the hyphen and has a third identity.

Beyond this re-definition, Arana's book about growing up in a bicultural family goes further. Discussion in the popular media about American identity has usually centered either on the whole society or on a particular ethnic group. The nature and challenge for the individual has largely been ignored. Arana's book, among other rich strands, addresses this unique challenge from an individual ethnic writer's point of view.

She, of course, rightly describes her memoir as a love story across a great ravine. In the 1940s her Peruvian father, an MIT-educated engineer, married a free-spirited, movie-star beautiful Wyoming musician and brought her back to his country to raise three children. The first chapters of the book narrate this sylvan childhood in Peru and reminds one of Sara Suleri's classic memoir *Meatless days* in her precocious account of a Pakistani father married to a Welsh mother in Lahore of the 1950s. Arana's parents' love for each other is fraught with tensions of two worlds colliding: her mother's free-spirited individualism clashes violently with her father's conservative, family orientation. Only the children formed a bicultural bridge between them.

She writes, "*A South American man, a North American woman hoping against hope, throwing a frail span over the divide, trying to bolt beams into sand. There was one large lesson they had yet to learn as they strode into the garden with friends, hungry for rum and fried blood.*" There is a fundamental rift between North and South America, a flaw so deep it is tectonic. The plates don't fit. The earth is loose. A fault runs through. Earthquakes happen. Walls are likely to fall.

> *The first chapters of the book narrate this sylvan childhood in Peru and reminds one of Sara Suleri's classic memoir* **Meatless days** *in her precocious account of a Pakistani father married to a Welsh mother in Lahore of the 1950s.*

Only when Arana came to live in America, however, she discovers that she is a hybrid. Confused by her identity she felt like a faker or a charlatan. Gradually she comes to terms with herself. As an American Chica she feels she does not lead a double life but a triple life in which she becomes a whole new person. She discovers she is a bridge-dweller: "*Venice may have its Bridge of Sighs, but there is another one in Lima 'Puente de Suspiros' and everytime I return to Peru, I find myself drawn to it, as if it holds some secret, some deeper meaning about life and love, I love to walk a bridge because I am neither gringa nor latina. The reality is I am a mongrel. I live on bridges, content with betwixt and between.*"

The metaphor of the bridge is central to this memoir. It cuts across heritages and appeals to a wide spectrum of immigrants in America. As a Pakistani-American living in the United States for the last 25 years, I too have felt similar emotions. The bridge connects points that might never have touched. It also enables you to connect across boundaries. While Arana's tries to mediate between and connect North with South, writers like me have tried to be mediators between the spheres of mutual ignorance between East and West. And sometimes in a rush of positive emotions have seen in their mind's eye the waters of Lahore's Ravi flow into Washington's Potomac.

The United States is now witnessing another great *mestizaje* similar to the one that fused the Spanish and Indian races. When today's Asian or Latino youngster wants to marry, he or she won't be bound by some tribal pressure towards endogamy. The prevalent practice is exogamy that is marrying outside your religious, ethnic or racial group which is a reversal of the notorious miscegenation laws that once existed in many states of the USA.

However, there are some extremists in America who feel that a multiethnic society is destroying the white, European soul of America, which is its true identity. In this context I asked Marie Arana whether the flowering of diversity that we have witnessed in the last two decades in the United States is irreversible? Would not another tragic catastrophe like 9/11 profoundly damage the future of a multicultural America?

In her response, she was optimistic. She explained that the uncertainty and unease of dealing with the "Other" that re- surfaced in America recently was a knee-jerk reaction to a shocking attack on this country. It was bound to be a temporary phenomenon. As time passes, all Americans will realize that the whole world has come to live in America and that we have to transcend bigotry and parochialism to survive.

> *As Richard Rodriguez has written, brown is not a singular color. Brown is evidence of mixture. Brown is a shade created by desire, an emblem of the erotic history of America which began the moment the African and the European met within the Indian eye.*

To sum up. Marie Arana's exquisite work on the complex nature of a bicultural self and the demands of a mixed heritage adeptly blends memoir with history. It is also a book about making a new world where all Americans, white, black or brown are learning to discover middle ground. After all tolerance is the specialty of bridge-dwellers and boundary-crossers.

As for the "browning of America", America has been brown for a long time. Actually it has been brown since its birth. As Richard Rodriguez has written, brown is not a singular color. Brown is evidence of mixture. Brown is a shade created by desire, an emblem of the erotic history of America which began the moment the African and the European met within the Indian eye.

Arana's love story of her parents is a testament to that universal love of the human race that knows no boundaries. (July 2002).

American Chica: two worlds, one childhood By Marie Arana .

The Dial Press, Random House, Inc, 1540 Broadway, New York, New York 10036. ISBN0-385-31962-2 309pp.

The Soros Doctrine

"AMERICA under Bush is a danger to the world," writes world renowned financier, author and philanthropist George Soros in his hurriedly-written new book *The Bubble of American Supremacy: Correcting the Misuse of Power*.

Soros has given away millions to promote open societies in more than 50 countries around the world. He has now committed more than 15 million dollars to the project of defeating President Bush in the forthcoming US presidential elections. A Hungarian Jew by birth, Soros survived the Nazi occupation and left communist Hungary in 1947 for England where he graduated from the London School of Economics. It was here that he came under the influence of Karl Popper's vision of the "open society" which became his political philosophy.

Soros came to settle in the US in 1956 and later as a financial speculator he made his legendary 1992 bet against the pound sterling bagging one billion dollars in profits within a few weeks. After he amassed a fortune of an estimated seven billion dollars he has become a unique kind of political philanthropist promoting freedom, human rights and democracy.

The Bubble of American Supremacy is Soros' eighth book. "*It is generally agreed,*" he writes, "*that September 11, 2001 changed the course of history. However, 9/11 could not have changed the course of history to the extent it has if President Bush had not responded the way he did.*"

According to Soros, the Bush administration proceeded to exploit the terrorist attack for its purposes whose underlying principles predated the tragedy. Those principles, he says, can be summed up as follows: international relations are relations of power, not law; power prevails and law legitimizes what prevails. This radical foreign policy, writes Soros, is part of a comprehensive ideology known as neo-conservatism or "a crude form of social Darwinism."

It was in June 2002 at West Point that the president enunciated the so-called "Bush Doctrine" which was based on two pillars: that the USA will do everything in its power to maintain its unquestioned military supremacy, and that the United States arrogates the right to pre-emptive action. In effect, writes Soros, this doctrine established two classes of sovereignty: the sovereignty of the United States, which takes precedence over international treaties and obligations; and the sovereignty of all other states, which is subject to the will of the United States. This, says Soros, is reminiscent of George Orwell's Animal Farm where all animals are equal, but some are more equal than others.

"To be sure," writes Soros, *"the Bush doctrine is not stated so starkly; it is shrouded in doublespeak. But when President Bush says, as he does frequently, that freedom will prevail (as in Iraq), he means that America will prevail."* In Soros' view, therefore, September 11 introduced a discontinuity into American foreign policy and the abnormal, the radical and the extreme have now become normal. As a result, more innocent people have been killed in Afghanistan and Iraq than were

"It is generally agreed," writes Soros, *"that September 11, 2001 changed the course of history. However, 9/11 could not have changed the course of history to the extent it has if President Bush had not responded the way he did."*

killed on September 11. He argues that the 9/11 attacks could have been treated as a crime against humanity rather than an act of war. *"What was needed was police work, not military action."*

Explaining the title of the book Soros believes that Bush's foreign policy comes from the same sort of "bubble" psychology that afflicted US financial markets in the late 1990s. He writes: *"They have used a real fact, our overwhelming military supremacy, to create a deluded worldview, that might makes right in the same way that the recent stock market boom used a real fact, the growth in technology, to lead to a delusion about the 'new economy.'"*

Some critics have called the title of the book and the above explanation a bit of a stretch. Amusingly, one of them questioned Soros' ability to predict the bursting of a political bubble, when he was unable to predict the bursting of the financial bubble during the dot com mania. Given Soros' penchant for things poetic it is true that he sometimes uses metaphors that lack clarity. For example, his use of philosophical jargon like "reflexivity", "radical fallibility", "fertile fallacies" and so on can confuse his readers. However, neither he nor his readers miss the bigger picture that this book paints quite clearly.

Notwithstanding hurried editing, the fundamental strength of Soros' book remains its powerful indictment of the Bush Doctrine. If anyone ever needed proof that this doctrine was flawed and misconceived, he states, the occupation of Iraq has already provided it.

It was last summer that Soros invited Democratic strategists to his house in Southampton, Long Island, including Clinton's chief of staff, John Podesta. There he proposed to mobilize voters against Bush in 17 battleground states by offering 15 million dollars. Now 15 million dollars is peanuts compared to Bush's re-election war chest of an estimated $200 million. But then money is not everything. Presidential contender, Dean, had 41 million dollars. And look what happened to him. What Democrats hope is that the American voters will see the dangers of the Bush Doctrine and realize the merits of replacing it with the something similar to a Soros Doctrine.

This latter doctrine, as detailed in the second half of Soros' book, will avoid pre-emptive military action and replace it with a collective approach to security. It will emphasize increased foreign aid. It will promote international cooperation and shun unilateralism. To deal with international terrorism and nuclear proliferation, in short, it will take multilateral preventive action of a constructive and affirmative nature like trying to understand the root causes of terrorism and then help alleviate them. **

Now if only Soros would bet his entire net worth of seven billion dollars to beat Bush? When asked this question, Soros is reported to have opened his mouth. Then closed it. Finally he replied: "If someone guaranteed it." (May 2004).

The Bubble of American Supremacy: Correcting the Misuse of Power
By George Soros Winsfield & Nicolson

**Although Bush won re-election in 2004 and Soros' candidate lost, Bush did tone down his "Doctrine" under a new Secretary of Defense and subsequently in 2008 with the election of Obama, for all intents and purposes, the Bush Doctrine was confined to the dustbin of history.

According to Soros, the Bush administration proceeded to exploit the 9/11 terrorist attack for its purposes whose underlying principles predated the tragedy. Those principles, he says, can be summed up as follows: international relations are relations of power, not law; power prevails and law legitimizes what prevails.

Book Review 4

American Plutocracy

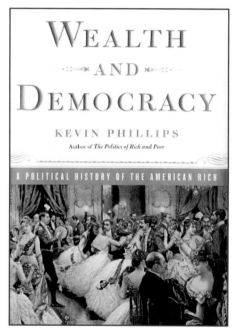

Kevin Phillips has been a thoughtful political and economic commentator for more than three decades. In 1969 he published his landmark book *The Emerging Republican Majority*. His bestseller *The Politics of Rich and Poor* was described as a "founding document" of the 1992 presidential election. In his latest book, *Wealth and Democracy: A Political History of the American Rich* he warns that America is fast becoming a plutocracy and the spirit of democracy is in decline. Nor does he believe America's international position to be secure.

He writes: that the US presents the "aging visage of the leading world economic power—purple-veined with years of high living, lips curled with the insolence of great wealth, eyes bloodshot with the late vigils of increasingly frequent financial crises." Most ominously, Phillips compares the US, post- September 11, to Holland in the early 1700s and Britain in the 20th century, when each nation, at the peak of its economic power, expended its energy and treasure in a burst of warfare leading to their decline as world powers.

Although this book is, at times, repetitive and the narrative is complex because it is more thematic than sequential, *Wealth and Democracy* is a book for our times. In ten fact-filled chapters, Phillips meticulously traces the phases of wealth concentration and the politics of the affluent from J.P. Morgan to Bill Gates and shows that the United States is in the grip of a rule of the rich controlled by Wall Street and big business.

According to the author, the rising inequality of incomes and wealth in America since the late 1970s has been striking, although few seem consciously aware of it. The wealthiest one per cent of households now own more than 40 per cent of all assets, including homes and financial investments (after deducting debt) — higher than in any year since 1929. On the other hand, the lowest 40 per cent of Americans own only one per cent of American assets.

Phillips compares the US, post-September 11, to Holland in the early 1700s and Britain in the 20th century, when each nation, at the peak of its economic power, expended its energy and treasure in a burst of warfare leading to their decline as world powers.

An important driver of this trend towards huge inequality, he says, is America's move from a manufacturing economy to an economy heavily dependent upon services, especially financial services. "So-called laissez faire is a pretence," he writes, "Government power and preferment have been used by the rich, not shunned." In sweeping terms, Phillips describes the consequences of this inequality. First, "financial corruption", the process by which wealthier Americans bent the rules of the economic system in pursuit of their own interest. The scandals in late 90's and early aughts at Enron, World Com, Merrill Lynch, Global Crossing, and elsewhere are examples of this mounting problem.

Second, Phillips talks of the political corruption that has come from a growing infusion of money into politics, both through campaign contributions and lobbying. This has resulted in a political system that is increasingly beholden to wealthy interests and gives less attention to the concerns of ordinary Americans.

Finally, Phillips talks of the cultural corruption that comes with great concentrations of wealth — namely, the fraying of America's social fabric and a culture that is highly materialistic and lacking in strong community values. Shockingly, according to Kevin Phillips, there's a parallel to the little known early 20th century domestic terrorism in America and to what happened on 9/11. In 1920, outside J.P. Morgan's bank, a 100-pound TNT bomb exploded: 38 bystanders killed, 200 maimed, a car tossed 20 feet in the air, windows of the Stock Exchange shattered. Evidence of the attack remains on what's still the Morgan Bank just blocks from 9/11's ground zero.

Writes Phillips: "Terrorism got started right after the first World War, and that's when all of this took place," he writes. "And I think we've seen something like that developing in the 1990s and now in the new century. It's a fierce reaction based on a sense that things are out of control and the power structure has gotten too rich and too remote." The great compassionate conservative, The Duchess of Windsor, once remarked: "You can never be too rich or too thin."

And that is precisely the most important insight in *Wealth and Democracy* when it reveals the central flaw in conservative mythology: wealth is not value.

Critics of Phillips' book — including an editorial in *Business Week* — while agreeing with his thesis that inequality in America has increased in the last two decades argue that the whole pie has also grown bigger. What they forget is at what cost? What about the $8 trillion household debt? What about the one billion dollars a day that US now needs to borrow from abroad to finance its current account deficit making it the largest debtor nation in the world? What happens when foreign creditors call in their loans?

> *In 1969, Phillips wrote about the failure of the liberal establishment because the Democrats broke their covenant with Middle America. Today it is the Republicans who starting with Reagan talked about the market and the promises of capitalism that have broken their covenant with Middle America.*

I agree with Phillips that when the US stock market has lost nearly $7 trillion in the last three years, without 9/11, President Bush would by now be in serious political trouble for weak and pro-corporate management of the economy. And that is the cautionary tale in *Wealth and Democracy*. The US government, he says, "concerned with protecting wealth may do at the expense of democratic procedures and may try to blame terrorism rather than flawed economic policy for hard times."

As America enters a fourth year with huge losses in the US financial markets and prepares for war with Iraq, Phillips believes that the United States is ripe for a historical correction. "As the 21st century gets under way, the imbalance of wealth and democracy in the US is unsustainable."

In 1969, Phillips wrote about the failure of the liberal establishment because the Democrats broke their covenant with Middle America. Today it is the Republicans who starting with Reagan talked about the market and the promises of capitalism that have broken their covenant with Middle America. And that is the key factor, which is bound to see a major reaction**.

(March 2003).

Wealth and Democracy: A Political History of the American Rich

By Kevin Phillips BroadwayBooks ISBN 0-7679-0533-4 473

Footnote: **That major historic reaction was the election of Barck Obama as Presdent of the United States as well as The House and Senate passing into the hands of the Democratic Party in 2008.

Globalization: The Great Myth

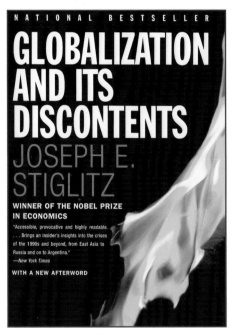

The predominant view among American economists and the media in general is that globalization — that is free trade, privatization and open markets — is both inevitable and beneficial. Even if globalization has flaws, the conventional opinion is that there is no better alternative. The best exposition of this optimistic view was laid out in Thomas Friedman's 2001 best seller *The Lexus and the Olive tree.*

In his recent book, *Globalization and its Discontents*, Joseph Stiglitz disagrees with this assessment. According to him globalization as understood in the West is a myth and the truth is that it is rigged in favor of rich nations. His criticism is the more telling because he won the Nobel Prize in Economics in 2001 and from 1993 to 2000 he was in a position to observe closely what was going on in Washington.

First, he was chairman of the President's Council of Economic Advisers and later chief economist of the World Bank, where rumor has it that former Treasury Secretary Larry Summers got him removed from office.

The main point of Stiglitz's book is that globalization has failed to help poor countries. In the last 10 years, poverty in Africa went up, not down and an average worker now earns one dollar per day. *"Critics of globalization accuse Western countries of hypocrisy,"* he writes, *"and the critics are right."* For example, he notes that industrialized countries have held on to their trade barriers on agricultural goods but forced developing nations to lower their tariffs. He narrates a startling story where a poor African country borrowed 100 million dollars at 18 per cent interest from a major US bank. Under IMF rules governing this loan, the African nation had to keep reserves with the

US treasury of an equal amount. Guess at what interest rate? Yes, at three per cent! So the poor nation borrowed $100 million dollars at 18 per cent but was paid three per cent for the so-called collateral.

The main culprit for destabilizing the economies of developing countries, therefore, according to Stiglitz is the IMF. This Washington institution which lends to troubled countries is a morass of political opportunism, ideologically motivated decision-making and bureaucratic inertia. IMF policies blatantly help US commercial and financial interests most notably Wall Street. In short, says the author, IMF remains an unabashed instrument of American foreign policy.

Joseph Stiglitz disagrees with the assessment of Friedman in his best seller "The Lexus and the Olive tree". According to Stiglitz, globalization as understood in the West is a myth and the truth is that it is rigged in favor of rich nations.

Stiglitz argues that IMF policies of fiscal austerity, privatization and market liberalization show little evidence of being an effective way of growth in developing countries. According to him deregulation cannot promote financial development when information is asymmetric and competition is inadequate. He calls the World Bank a "learning organization" but describes the IMF as "learning impaired". He argues that the IMF needs to develop a culture of openness that encourages debate, dissent and learning.

Currently, says Stiglitz, the IMF is run by international civil servants who have to choose between dissent and professional advancement. He is furious when he talks about top officials of the IMF who end up going to work for large US financial institutions. For example, Stanley Fischer, deputy managing director at the IMF, during the 1998 Asian and Russian crises, is today vice-chairman at Citigroup. "One could only ask" writes Stiglitz, "was Fischer being richly rewarded for having faithfully executed what he was told to do?"

Unless the IMF is reformed as an institution, Stiglitz sees no escape from rampant ignorance and incredible secrecy. Imagine there is no freedom of information act applicable here and even members of US Congress are not officially privy to how some financial decisions are reached. The author calls for greater transparency and increased accountability at this all-powerful organization which, according to him, has doomed globalization.

The crux of Stiglitz's message, therefore, is that growth in developing countries can evolve more in harmony with local conditions and not on Washington's calendar nor on simplistic, mandatory doctrines as practiced by IMF which invariably "beggars" them. When a developing country faces a recession, he suggests keeping interest rates low instead of raising them thus avoiding a financial meltdown. It is also imperative, he says, to keep credit flowing, rather than closing the banks as IMF did on more than one occasion.

Given this analysis, no wonder the world as a whole has not seen the benefits of globalization. Some two billion people today live in countries where economic growth has stagnated and poverty is on the rise. One could even argue that these countries have become less and less globalized. For them what is eulogized as globalization is just an illusion. Most people in Latin America, the Middle East and Central Asia are poorer today than they were in 1990. The average per capita income of Muslim countries — from Morocco to Bangladesh — is now just half the world's average.

> *The crux of Stiglitz's message is that growth in developing countries can evolve more in harmony with local conditions and not on Washington's calendar nor on simplistic, mandatory doctrines as practiced by IMF which invariably "beggars" them.*

Informed people in the West are beginning to realize that poverty is not only a matter of income; it also manifests itself in powerlessness, isolation, despair and terrorism. Since the logic of pure capitalism does not favor social justice, economic globalization has become a formidable cause of inequality among nations. Instead of using globalization as a mask for US hegemony, restraint and magnanimity could prove to be successful statecraft for the greater good of all mankind.

Since the US has no rival in any critical dimensions of power, there is always a temptation to exploit the uni-polar world order as it obtains today and become a global bully. In the words of Stiglitz: *"We have focused so hard on our own economic mythology and on managing globalization to our short term benefit that we have been blind to what we are doing to ourselves and the world."* (October 2002).

Globalization and its Discontents By Joseph E. Stiglitz

W.W. Norton and Company Inc., New York. ISBN 0393051242. 192pp.

Another Evil Empire?

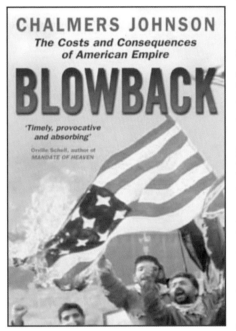

"WE Americans deeply believe that our role in the world is virtuous — that our actions are almost invariably for the good of others as well as ourselves. Even when our actions have led to disaster, we assume that the motives behind them were honorable."

So writes Chalmers Johnson in his book *Blowback: the cost and consequences of American Empire.*

A one-time supporter of the Vietnam war, Johnson — who is an expert on China and Japan — now believes, *"the evidence is building up that in the decade following the end of the cold war, the United States has largely abandoned a reliance on diplomacy, economic aid, international law, and multilateral institutions in carrying out its foreign policies and resorted much of the time to bluster, military force, and financial manipulation."*

Blowback was first published in hardcover in March 2000 and, like Ahmed Rashid's book *Taliban*, was mostly ignored by the US media in the pre-9/11 go-go years. The few reviews that did appear in the Foreign Affairs Quarterly or The New York Times dubbed it as "a comic book" or "a book marred by an over-riding, sweeping and cranky one- sidedness." After 9/11, however, the book has hit the best-seller list and is now in its fourth reprinting in paperback. Some critics now hail it as "brilliant" and "stunning."

The neologism 'blowback' was first coined by the CIA in March 1954 in a recently declassified report on the 1953 operation to overthrow the government of Mossadegh in Iran. It is a metaphor for the unintended consequences of the US government's international activities that have been kept secret from the American people. Johnson lists, among others, the illegal drug trade as a result of US support for dictatorships in Latin America, Khomeini's Islamic revolution in Iran due to US support for the repressive regime of the Shah for 25 years, the massacres inflicted in Cambodia by Pol Pot as a byproduct of the war in Vietnam, the 1991 Gulf War as a result of US early support for Saddam Hussain, the bombing of USS Cole and the Twin Towers in New York in 1993, the rise of the Taliban in Afghanistan in 1996 all due to the US Afghan war against the Soviet Union as examples of blowback.

The book, which is actually Asia-centric, discusses chapter by chapter various East Asian countries where the US organized a military security system since 1950 to contain communism. From a highly critical viewpoint, Johnson examines American military presence in Japan, Korea, Okinawa, Taiwan, Philippines and Indonesia. That the US has not significantly reduced or adjusted its military position after the fall of the Soviet Union reveals to the author America's commitment to military-economic imperialism. From the rape of a 12 year old girl by US marines in Okinawa to imposition of economic austerity in Indonesia by the IMF (followed by a quick purchase of its industrial plants on easy terms by American corporations) Johnson sees the imperialist mentality as the defining style of American actions and expectations abroad.

Blowback was first published in hardcover in March 2000 and, like Ahmed Rashid's book "Taliban", was mostly ignored by the US media in the pre-9/11 go-go years. The few reviews that did appear in the Foreign Affairs Quarterly or The New York Times dubbed it as "a comic book" or "a book marred by an over-riding, sweeping and cranky one-sidedness."

Observes Johnson: *"Okinawa is still essentially a military colony of the Pentagon. It is used to project American power throughout Asia in the service of a de facto US grand strategy to perpetuate or increase American hegemonic power in this crucial region."*

Blowback is therefore a call for the US to re-think its position in the world and to disengage from many of its global commitments. In 2001, according to the author, the US had 200,000 troops stationed at 65 military bases in 40 countries. Johnson urges the dismantling of West Bank Israeli settlements as fast as possible and the withdrawal of US troops from Saudi Arabia. In Okinawa, where the US has 38 military bases in the midst of 1.3 million civilians, he wants America to bring home the Third Marine Division.

> *The neologism 'blowback' was first coined by the CIA in March 1954 after the overthrow of Mossadegh in Iran. It is a metaphor for the unintended consequences of the US government's international activities that have been kept secret from the American people.*

In a subsequent post-9/11 article published in the left- leaning magazine, *The Nation*, Johnson wrote: "The suicidal assassins of September 11, 2002 did not 'attack America', as our political leaders and the news media like to maintain; they attacked American foreign policy."

He went on to say that to portray the 9/11 attacks as a "clash of civilizations" or as President Bush termed it as "good versus evil" was a meaningless post-cold war American jargon. "Not only was this disingenuous," he wrote, "but it was also an attempt to evade responsibility for the blowback that American imperial projects have generated."

Needless to say, Chalmers Johnson leftist writings are quite impressive and have a ring of truth to them. Unfortunately, however, sometimes he does sound "cranky" when he advocates "disappearance from the earth of the most corrupt capital in the western hemisphere" — meaning Washington D.C.

In Blowback, Johnson clearly recycles a conceptual framework for analyzing US foreign policy that has been extensively articulated for more than three decades in the writings of Noam Chomsky: *At War with Asia* (1970), *For Reasons of State* (1973), *Of Power and Ideology* (1986), *Towards a New Cold War* (1988); *Deterring Democracy* (1991) *to name only a few.*

But Chomsky is never cited in *Blowback*, nor do any of his works appear in Johnson's bibliography. Furthermore, Johnson finds American hubris responsible for practically everything he dislikes. He never gives America credit for anything that has gone right like progress towards democracy in South Korea or Taiwan nor the economic miracle of Japan after World War II. And then there is the abject failure of the left in American politics.. The venom of the left's political discourse dogmatically assumes that the other side is not just wrong but dumb. (December 2002)

Blowback: the Costs and Consequences of American Empire

By Chalmers Johnson Time Warner. ISBN: 0-7515-3080-8 289pp.

Book Review 7

Western Purblindness

DAVID Hirst, a former Middle East correspondent of the Guardian newspaper, wrote *The Gun and the Olive Branch* originally in 1977. This was the eve of the historic breakthrough in the Middle East conflict and the time when Sadat made his peace-making journey to Jerusalem. However, the book was largely ignored by the US media with what Hirst later called "a resounding and puzzling silence". Only The Washington Post noticed the book but wrote a brief, derisive review. Later, the editor of *The New Republic* called the second edition "the most malignantly anti-Israel book ever published. "

Today if you look at the Amazon.com website you will find "readers" screaming that it is "a ridiculous book" or "Hirst needs total re-education" or even "please read something else." Rumor has it that in the past the book disappeared from bookshops and libraries in America and to purchase it cost a fortune.

Anyway, the first edition of *The Gun and the Olive Branch*, which caused a storm in the rest of the world 26 years ago, had just nine chapters. These chapters provided a well-documented historical panorama beginning with the 1880s, when world Zionism began purchasing land in Palestine to settle European Jews, to the 1967 Six-day War in pursuit of a greater Israel. Exposing the twists and turns of political intrigue in London, Washington, Tel Aviv and elsewhere the book concluded that Zionism was simply the West's last colonial enterprise, establishing the Jewish state in 1948 through the "ethnic cleansing" of the Palestinians and then defiantly opposing the normal imperial pattern of relinquishing control to the indigenous population.

In the second edition of the book published in 1983 David Hirst added three chapters detailing the Egypt-Israel peace agreement, the subsequent "rape" of the West Bank, Israeli invasion of Lebanon and the resignation of Prime Minister Begin.

> *The basic thesis of the book is that the Zionists have been gobbling Palestine from the Arabs a little bit at a time for about one hundred years, and they are still doing it and that is the principal cause of violence in Palestine.*

The third edition of the book published in August 2003 updates the tragic history of the Middle East. In addition to the 12 chapters of the earlier books, it has a 130-page foreword, which highlights developments like Likud's rise, the growing power of the Israeli lobby in the United States, two *intifadas* and the ominous rise of suicide bombers, countless diplomatic attempts like the Oslo peace process, Israeli occupation of the West Bank and Gaza, the rise of Jewish settlements in occupied territories, the growth of dissent in Israel, the showdown between Sharon and Arafat and the possibility of nuclear catastrophe that threatens the Middle East.

This foreword has a tone, which is even darker than the original book. The basic thesis is the same, i.e., that the Zionists have been gobbling Palestine from the Arabs a little bit at a time for about one hundred years, and they are still doing it and that is the principal cause of violence in Palestine. This colonial enterprise, adds Hirst, depends for its very existence on the support of an imperial sponsor. First that sponsor was Great Britain when we had the infamous Balfour Declaration in 1917. By 1948 the sponsorship shifted to the newly emergent superpower, the USA.

"Hence," writes Hirst, "the Palestinian tragedy has taken place in the 20th century as Western Purblindness — an indispensable environment for the actualization of the Zionist venture." This purblindness continues till present day. Witness the recent war in Iraq, writes Hirst. The current American administration's neo-cons saw the road to war in Iraq no longer through peace in Palestine; peace in Palestine was seen through the war on Baghdad. Under the pretext of disarming Iraq of its imaginary WMD's, the USA was not merely adopting Israel's belligerent methods of preemption, it was also adopting Israel's enemies as its own.

What will be the consequences of this neo-conservative blueprint for the Middle East, asks Hirst. His response: The path chosen by the Bush administration has calamity written all over it. When Bush calls Sharon a 'man of peace' and dismisses Arafat's historic peace offer in which he renounced 78 per cent of Palestinian territory, it is nothing but a tragedy on a monumental scale and could lead to nuclear war down the road.

It is true that this classic book is a trenchant history of the Arab-Israeli conflict. But given the stark one-sidedness of a majority of the American media, academics and politicians, *The Gun and the Olive Branch* is a corrective work. It is clearly pro-Arab and therefore provides some balance to the dominant orthodoxy of the "friends of Israel" in America.

The main shortcoming of the book is that it is written by a journalist who relies on second hand sources. However, Hirst has a broad view of things and his main objective is to expose the myopia of the other side. Obviously, his conclusions and assertions should by no means be accepted wholesale. Unfortunately, this problem exists with any sympathetic historian.

I always remind people of what Oscar Wilde once said: "History proves that anything can be proved by history." Recently when the Democratic Presidential candidate Howard Dean said, in passing, that American foreign policy should be "even-handed" between Israel and the Palestinians, there was such uproar in the US that the beleaguered candidate had to apologize and withdraw his statement almost immediately. Given this state of amnesia and intolerance, if Hirst's book is ignored again, it is ignored at the world's own collective peril. (December 2003).

The Gun and the Olive Branch: The Roots of Violence in the Middle East
By David Hirst

> *It is true that this classic book is a trenchant history of the Arab-Israeli conflict. But given the stark one-sidedness of a majority of the American media, academics and politicians, The Gun and the Olive Branch is a corrective work.*

Continental Drift

While extolling the virtues of American imperialism, the central thesis of Robert Kagan's recent bestseller, *Of Paradise and Power* is that the "power gap" between the US and Europe is now so vast that there is "little use in thinking of them as partners in the new world order."

This manifesto-style slim book is an expanded version of an essay originally published as "Power and weakness" in *Policy Review*, the right-wing Hoover Institute's bi-monthly magazine.

Kagan, a conservative think-tanker, is a senior associate at the Carnegie Endowment and is the author of *A Twilight Struggle: American Power and Nicaragua*. He lives in Brussels. Before and during the just concluded Iraq war, this book has generated much heat and controversy in the US. It is now on the bestseller list. Some conservative foreign policy mavens have compared it to George F. Kennan's 1947 essay in Foreign Affairs advocating containment of the Soviet Union. Kissinger has called it a "seminal treatise," but liberals like Gore Vidal describe Kagan as "being in the grip of most unseemly megalomania, speaking for no one but political hustlers within the Washington beltway".

In his book Kagan writes, "*It is time to stop pretending that Europeans and Americans share a common view of the world, or even that they occupy the same world. On the all-important question of power, American and European perspectives are diverging.*" According to him, Europe is moving "*beyond power*" into a "*self-contained world of laws and rules and transnational negotiation and cooperation*". It is entering a post-historical paradise of peace, what Kant called "Perpetual Peace".

The United States, meanwhile, adds Kagan, "*remains mired in history, exercising power in the anarchic Hobbesian world where international laws and rules are unreliable and where true security and the defense and promotion of a liberal order still depend on the possession and use of military might*". That is why on major international questions today, *"Americans are from Mars and Europeans are from Venus: They agree on little and understand one another less and less."* Kagan says that this Euro-American split is not transitory - the product of one American election of a conservative President or one catastrophic event like 9/11. The reasons for the transatlantic divide are deep, long in development, and likely to endure.

According to Kagan it was the demise of the Soviet Union and the birth of the "unipolar moment" that made United States more willing to use force abroad. He denies that 9/11 is at the heart of America's aggressive posture. He points out that whereas the combined military budgets of all European countries is around 150 billion dollars, USA's annual military budget is already $450 billion and climbing. No wonder, therefore, the 1990's saw the French coin the term "hyperpuissance" or hyperpower to describe the American behemoth too worryingly powerful to be called merely a superpower.

Kissinger has called this book a "seminal treatise," but Gore Vidal describe Kagan as "being in the grip of most unseemly megalomania, speaking for no one but political hustlers within the Washington beltway."

And this process, says Kagan started not with Bush but during the Clinton presidency when Europeans began to complain about being lectured by the "hectoring hegemon". According to Kagan, therefore, Europeans have a deep interest in devaluing and eventually eradicating the brutal laws of an anarchic, Hobbesian world where power is the ultimate determinant. This is no reproach, writes Kagan. It is what weaker powers have wanted from time immemorial. It was what a weak America wanted in the eighteenth and early nineteenth centuries, when the brutality of a European system of power politics run by the global giants of France, Britain, and Russia left Americans constantly vulnerable to imperial thrashing. It was what the other small powers of Europe wanted in those years, too, only to be sneered at by Bourbon kings and other powerful monarchs, who spoke instead of *raison d'etat*.

In other words, shorn of euphemisms and obfuscation, Kagan's justification for the use of overwhelming force against an impoverished country like Iraq by the United States is that since Europe in its glory days indulged in colonialism and pillage of weaker powers, so too should America today.

His conclusion is dumbfounding: *"Europe should let us do what we must to keep the peace, recognizing that we have just entered a long era of American hegemony."* Fortunately, wiser heads in America have challenged these dangerous imperial delusions. Farsighted Americans like former President Carter, George McGovern or Daniel Ellsberg not only opposed the Iraq war, but expressed views that are indistinguishable from Kagan's Europeans.

Secondly, Kagan's singular focus on the military foundations of power is truly troublesome. He fails to understand that brute force never results in lasting security. The more America resorts to force, the more it will be disliked, the weaker it will become politically. "Regime change" through force is relatively easy; what is difficult, as time will tell, is "nation building". History teaches us that Mr Big always invites his own demise. That is what happened to Napoleon, to Hitler and to Stalin. One of the oldest rules of history is that power begets superior counter-power.

Thirdly, in America's war against terrorism, it should be remembered that terror will not be defeated with drones, F-16s and smart weapons. It will be defeated with justice, humility, compassion, friendship, respect for cultural diversity, reverence for world faiths and love for humanity and international law.

In his forthcoming brilliant book, *The Unconquerable World*, Jonathan Schell writes: *"The days when humanity can hope to save itself from force with force are over. None of the known international structures of force — not the balance of power, not the balance of terror, not empire — can rescue the world from brutality and annihilation. Only the cooperative structures of power based on diplomacy, economic welfare and international law offer hope."*

Needless to say, having suffered two World Wars and millions of dead, Europe, which has now chosen the cooperative structures of power for itself, offers a more rational approach to world order. Contrary to what Kagan preaches, it is Europe that is ideally placed to be a model of peace and democracy for the world in the 21st century. (June 2003).

Of Paradise and Power: America and Europe in the New World Order By Robert Kagan Alfred A. Knopf   ISBN 1-4000-4093-0 103pp.

Shorn of euphemisms and obfuscation, Kagan's justification for the use of overwhelming force against an impoverished country like Iraq by the United States is that since Europe in its glory days indulged in colonialism and pillage of weaker powers, so too should America today.

Age of Terror

THE AGE OF TERROR

AMERICA AND THE WORLD AFTER SEPTEMBER 11

PAUL KENNEDY · NIALL FERGUSON
JOHN LEWIS GADDIS · MAXINE SINGER
ABBAS AMANAT · HAROLD HONGJU KOH
CHARLES HILL · PAUL BRACKEN

Edited by STROBE TALBOTT and NAYAN CHANDA

At a time of broad reassessment of security, business and other policies, six Yale University scholars and practitioners of international affairs, joined by two other leading scholars in international relations, security and science analyze the implications of 9/11 in America and beyond in their book *The Age of Terror*. The book is edited by Strobe Talbott, a former Deputy Secretary of State and now director of Yale's Centre for the study of globalization, and Nayan Chanda, a longtime editor at *The Far Eastern Economic Review*.

It is not an exaggeration to state that prior to September 11, the word Afghan to most Americans meant no more than a handmade rug. Even for experienced Western columnists this attack on American soil — which literally came out of the blue — created an unprecedented problem. What was published here in the immediate aftermath of September 11 was, therefore, intellectually incoherent and emotionally confusing.

To say that the leadership of America was unprepared would be a monumental understatement. By characterizing this attack as simply "good versus evil," they resorted to a template for bygone wars like the struggle between the Allies and the Axis Powers in the Second World War. As Strobe Talbott points out in the introduction to *The Age of Terror*, Al Qaida was the "ultimate NGO", without a flag or an army to speak of. Besides, the attack on the Twin Towers was like a Hollywood movie mass murder as performance art. In this startling backdrop what was needed was much new thinking. The way the attack was organized by decentralized, suicide terrorists living in America, using civilian aircraft and low tech weapons made both the nature of this crisis bewildering and its solution beyond comprehension.

This book, therefore, in its eight essays grapples with the question of how and why did September 11 happen and what did it mean for the future of America and the world? Although four essays by Bracken, Kennedy, Singer and Koh in this book do provide useful observations ranging from the changing nature of future wars, the failure of American intelligence, the threat of biological terrorism and the challenge to preserve human rights and American values in the new environment, these pieces are full of platitudes and resemble Op-Ed pages. The fifth essay by Charles Hill is just plain invective rather than reasoned arguments.

> *This book in its eight essays grapples with the question of how and why did September 11 happen and what did it mean for the future of America and the world?*

However, three essays by Gaddis, Amanat and Ferguson, which are worth discussing, do provide informed, original opinion. John Gaddis, professor of history at Yale, offers three important lessons for America's policy makers. First, the geographical position and military power of the US are no longer by themselves sufficient to ensure its security. Secondly, American foreign policy of unilateralism in the post-cold war era had failed to serve "our interests". This era of a single superpower with its self-indulgence and talk of end of history was now facing the dark side of globalization. Third, to correct this failure of strategic vision where "our power exceeded our wisdom", the USA must now look into the conditions that breed terrorism in so many parts of what we used to call the "third" world.

Abbas Amanat, professor of modern Middle East at Yale, in his piece "Re-inventing of Islamic extremism" states that although to some in the West, September 11 was a confirmation of their worst fears of stereotyped Islam, the presence of many Muslim communities in the Western countries has had an educational and salutary effect on them. These communities show Osama bin Laden as a grotesque anomaly. Apart from a brilliant discussion on the political uses of martyrdom in Shia Islam and its recent re-invention in the Iraq-Iran war, Amanat traces the roots of Islamic extremism to the Muslim experience of European colonialism and its aftermath.

Since 1945, he points out, ten all-out wars have taken place in the region between Egypt and Afghanistan and, by and large, the US has been at the heart of these conflicts, some because of its unconditional support of Israel. The result is that along with long visa lines at American embassies in Middle Eastern countries, a profound mistrust of America has also grown. After 9/11, Amanat says that America can no longer treat the Middle East merely in terms of their available energy sources and strategic value. To ensure its own security, America must join hands with moderates living in the Islamic world and promote peace, economic development and democracy.

The third interesting essay in this book is by Niall Ferguson, professor of Political and Financial history at Oxford, entitled "Clashing civilizations or mad mullahs?" He states that in order to counter Osama's nihilistic "Islamo-Bolshevism," America should embark on a campaign of benign imperialism like it successfully did after the Second World War in Japan and Germany. America can develop institutional foundations of

> *Even the best writing in this book offers only few answers on how to deal with the complex challenges that lie ahead for American policy makers.*

law and order in today's rogue states to make the world safe for capitalism and democracy. Ferguson finds talk of the third world war today as absurd because there was no clash of civilizations like the one that occurred during the second world war. He sees Islamic fundamentalism creating more of a centrifugal rather than centripetal effect and a continued process of disintegration resulting in religious and ethnic civil wars like we have recently had in Yugoslavia, Iraq, Afghanistan, Somalia and Sierra Leone.

Finally, Charles Hill's jingoistic essay sticks out like a sore thumb in this book of reasoned arguments. Hill is a former Kissinger aide and his angry rant against Arab governments and the Clinton administration in failing to control Osama belies the fact that what happened on September 11 was in part a blowback from the practice of *realpolitik* by successive Republican administrations. After all, Osama was President Reagan's ultimate freedom fighter.

Most essays in the *The Age of Terror* leave little doubt that the fall of the Twin Towers in New York will prove as consequential as the fall of the Berlin Wall. With weapons of mass destruction lot cheaper to obtain, the danger is that the worse is still to come. However, even the best writing in this book offers only few answers on how to deal with the complex challenges that lie ahead for American policy makers. Washington is bound to be faced with conflicting imperatives, which will require wisdom and statesmanship to untangle.   (March 2002)

The Age of Terror: America and the World after September 11.

Edited by Strobe Talbott and Nayan Chanda

Basic Books distributed by HarperCollins   ISBN 0-465-08356-0 224pp.

Rumsfeld: An Overwrought Panegyric

Rumsfeld: Greeting Sadam Hussain.

Midge Decter's *Rumsfeld: A Personal Portrait* is a superficial book which does not do justice to the complex, paradoxical, over-confident and controversial personality of America's current defense secretary.

According to the book description printed on the hardcover jacket "Drawing on her long acquaintance with Rumsfeld, a wealth of documents, and interviews with him and his family, friends, and colleagues, Midge Decter provides riveting accounts of the many milestones marking the journey Rumsfeld made from the suburbs of Chicago to the Pentagon."

On the contrary the author does not provide any fresh information beyond Rumsfeld's well-known ascent from a congressman from Chicago to White House Chief of Staff under President Ford to the architect of President Bush's global war on terror.

As we know, Decter is a member of the board of the ultra-conservative Heritage Foundation and wife of Norman Podhoretz an editor, and a neoconservative polemicist.

Although a celebrity puff book like this one is typically bought in bulk by right wing think tanks and other organizations to enable it to crack the bestseller list, this book received no major reviews anywhere in the American media, sold dismally in the real marketplace and does not even have an index.

Although the book has $24.95 as its retail price, you can buy it for $3.00. Now, sale price may not be the sole criterion of the quality of a book, but I must confess that this book is what we in South Asia call a "Qasida" or a panegyric and the naive way it attempts to portray Rumsfeld as an 'American icon' is just plain hilarious.

One reader on a famous American bookstore's website wrote: "Simpering... fawning.... worshipful... grotesque... deranged... a few of the adjectives that immediately come to mind upon finishing this book. Ultimately, I found Decter's embarrassingly obsessive hyperbole to be profoundly distasteful."

Another left-wing critic went even further: *"Perhaps this poor woman is experiencing a much-delayed second (or third) childhood and Donald Rumsfeld awakens in her the kind of turbulent and pubescent obsession that she once swooned out for her father or Elvis Presley. You can wring this book out like a sponge and be delivered of at least 2-1/2 gallons of saccharine necon whitewash and laughable spew."*

Now I would not disparage this book to that extent. It does have its entertainment value. For instance, Decter praises Donald Rumsfeld as if he was a Greek God and that many elegant, New York socialites hang Rumsfeld's picture in their dressing rooms. Such a paean to the God Apollo, as it were, makes the book transforms itself into surreal fun. To add to the wonders of this book, there are dozens of photographs which, to say the least, are a real treat. There is Rumsfeld, the boxer and the football-hero in his youth. There is Rumsfeld flying a B-1 bomber 'to prove its reliability!' And so on.

> *Decter does not provide any fresh information beyond Rumsfeld's well-known ascent from a congressman from Chicago to White House Chief of Staff under President Ford to the architect of President Bush's global war on terror.*

Yes we know that this is a "personal portrait" and not an objective study. Yet the point is that at a time when the world faces a global war on terrorism, when "The Washington Post" reports that military families in America are protesting "the snuffing out of precious lives of their loved ones in a meaningless war in Iraq", when according to "The New York Times" there is increasingly the cataclysmic possibility of a nuclear 9/11 in America, to dole out an overwrought eulogy trivializes a major figure who is the prime mover of an arrogant, unilateralist US foreign policy and responsible for the life, death and future of millions.

As Pakistan's charge d'affaires in Brussels I had the chance of meeting Rumsfeld at a Belgian Foreign Minister's lunch in 1973 at Palais de Gulois in Brussels when he was US ambassador to NATO. Needless to say, even at a young age he struck one as fascinating. But that is not all.

Readers who want to understand the real Donald Rumsfeld must read a forthcoming book in April 2004 by James Mann entitled "*Rise of the Vulcans: The history of Bush's War Cabinet.*" Excerpts of this book have appeared in The Atlantic Monthly magazine of November 2003 and March 2004.

> *I must confess that this book is what we in South Asia call a "Qasida" or a panegyric and the naive way it attempts to portray Rumsfeld as an 'American icon' is just plain hilarious.*

In these excerpts we find that Rumsfeld has been involved with the highest reaches of power in the US government for over three decades so much so that in 1973 he hired a young aide named Richard Cheney. Writes Mann: "*Thirty years ago he was lot like the man we know today—a divisive figure who relished bureaucratic combat, aimed to shake the established order, and was tenaciously committed to his own ideas and ambitions.*" However, what is surprising to know is that during the Nixon administration, although young Rumsfeld was a mid-westerner he was not only a moderate but even liberal.

In Mann's book we will also discover that during the Reagan administration, Rumsfeld and Cheney were key players in a clandestine program to install a new "President" in the event a nuclear attack killed the country's leaders. According to Mann, these two powerful men are " *a part of the permanent hidden national-security apparatus of the Unites States—inhabitants of a world in which Presidents come and go, but America keeps on fighting.*"

Finally, no study of America's Defense Secretary is complete without noting that he is also a poet. However his poetry is like the man, paradoxical. As Hart Seely has written in his book "The Poetry of Rumsfeld" , he never faces the subject head on but weaves away, letting inversion and repetitions confuse and beguile. Here is an excerpt from DOD news briefing Feb. 12, 2002:

The Unknown as we know,
There are known knowns.
There are things we know we know.
We also know There are known unknowns.
That is to say
We know there are some things We do not know.
But there are also unknown unknowns,
The ones we don't know We don't know.

(May 2004).

Rumsfeld: A Personal Portrait By Midge Decter

Publisher: Harper Collins 2003   ISBN# 0-06-056091-6

Update:

In July 2013, Rumsfeld published a little book of aphorisms on how to run Washington, and therefore, the world, titled: *Rumsfeld's Rules*.

One of the rules states: *"The only stupidities that are not easily solved are those created by very intelligent men."*

Go figure.

According to Mann, Cheney and Rumsfeld are " a part of the permanent hidden national-security apparatus of the Unites States— inhabitants of a world in which Presidents come and go, but America keeps on fighting."

Ode to War

THE main thesis of Robert Kaplan's new book *Warrior Politics: Why Leadership demands a Pagan Ethos* is what amoral ancient historians and thinkers have to teach contemporary American leaders about conducting foreign policy in a dangerous world.

In this scary little book, Kaplan argues that many old lessons have to be re-learned, chiefly the need for and moral uses of war as informed by the works of Livy, Thucydides, Sun-Tzu, Machiavelli, Hobbes and Churchill.

In less than 200 pages, *Warrior Politics* takes the reader from ancient Sumer to the Serbia of the 1990s, arguing that while times may change, human nature does not. He echoes his guru, the conservative Harvard Professor, Sam Huntington, who in his *The Soldier and the State* had said: "*Military leaders had to take for granted — and anticipate — the irrationality, weakness and evil in human nature*". Thus foreign policy today had to be conducted "only in terms of worst-case scenarios" where power has precedence over virtue, and pragmatism over idealism.

In his opening chapter entitled "There is no modern world", Kaplan points out that the post-colonial era is only in the early stages of collapse. For the time being, only marginal states like Somalia and Sierra Leone have broken down. In the next decade, much larger countries, more populous and urbanized, like Nigeria and Pakistan may crumble. Today, owing to technological advancement, globalization and low-end urbanization there is the birth of a new warrior class which comes from hundreds of millions of unemployed young males in the developing world.

"*I saw first hand,*" writes Kaplan, "*the creation of these warriors at Islamic schools in Pakistani slums.*" Therefore, he warns American leaders to be prepared. "*If our soldiers cannot fight and kill at close range our status as superpower is in question.*" We must heed the lessons of history and unlike ancient Troy do not try to appease our enemies in the false belief that our wealth and success would buy peace. In other words, only all-out war is the solution to crush the increasingly cruel and martyrdom-seeking third world warriors.

Kaplan quotes Achilles with relish: *"What I really crave is slaughter and blood and choking groans of men."* Having said that, *Warrior Politics* embarks on a pseudo-scholarly journey of glorifying war and realpolitik. From Machiavelli, Kaplan gleans that the Judeo-Christian private morality is hypocritical. Instead it is the morality of results that is true public virtue, no matter it may be pagan. From Livy's Punic wars he discovers that the vigor to face our adversaries must ultimately come from pride in our past achievements. Sun-Tzu's *The Art of Warfare* and Thucydides *Peloponnesian War* teach Kaplan the central thought that war is not an aberration. Finally, Churchill's river war against the Mahdi in Sudan in 1899 exposed the ancient world within the modern one.

As I read this book and its dubious odes to war, I came to realize what really constitutes the mind of a fundamentalist, not what he is thinking but how. Surely Osama bin Laden must be thinking the same so-called ancient truths and virtues when he ordered his attack on New York and Washington DC.

It is a tragedy that with 9/11, books like *Warrior Politics* are receiving kudos in America today as "prescient". Someone has to step in and prevent this war between fundamentalists. Human nature is not necessarily evil. Historicism begun by Hegel, modified by Marx and now manifest in post-modernism, clearly shows that human nature is not something immutable but is pliable and mostly an artifact of history, culture and language.

> *Kaplan echoes his guru, the conservative Harvard Professor, Sam Huntington, who in his "The Soldier and the State" had said: "Military leaders had to take for granted — and anticipate — the irrationality, weakness and evil in human nature."*

Despite a valiant effort at studying Machiavelli and Hobbes, Kaplan has failed to distinguish between selfishness (as Hobbes understood it as ignoring the interest of others) and self-interest (which is a far more complex action as Machiavelli understood it). The fact of the matter is that Kaplan's historical gleanings in this book are suspiciously convenient and brief to build a general theory on. To draw conclusions about 3000 years of human history and then build theories about the past and future upon them requires more reading and thinking than Kaplan appears to have done in this slim volume.

For example, witness again the lack of any evidence or good argument when he states that *"liberty grew in the west mainly because it served the interests of power"*. On the contrary, as was pointed out by Donald Kagan in *The New York Times*, it was the lack of a dominant imperial power in Europe owing to geographically separated weak rulers and the struggle between the church and the state that resulted in the emergence of freedom.

Warrior Politics is a flawed book even though it comes from an influential reporter who is a senior correspondent of *The Atlantic Monthly*. Although he has written nine books in the last 14 years, Kaplan has over-reached his scholarly pretensions in his latest publication.

Kaplan enjoys great standing with the American leadership in power and has been invited to brief Republican presidents who patronize him. But American policymakers will be better served if, instead, they read two recent books that provide genuine constructive thinking after 9/11: *The Paradox of American Power* by Joseph Nye, a former Clinton administration official, which cautions against an arrogant, unilateral employment of military power and *On globalization* by George Soros which provides a detailed economic plan for creating the much needed safety nets like health care, education and unemployment benefits for the hundreds of millions of jobless youth of the developing world so that they too have a stake in a civilized life. (April 2002).

Warrior Politics: Why Leadership demands a Pagan Ethos

By Robert Kaplan   ISBN 0375505636   Random House

Despite a valiant effort at studying Machiavelli and Hobbes, Kaplan has failed to distinguish between selfishness (as Hobbes understood it as ignoring the interest of others) and self-interest (which is a far more complex action as Machiavelli understood it).

Book Review 12

Still the White Man's Burden?

The 'pluralism versus assimilation' debate has raged in the US for nearly 200 years. In his new book *The Death of the West: how dying populations and immigrant invasions imperil our country and civilization*, Pat Buchanan, therefore, gives much old news. However, there is a particular spin in this book. Buchanan wages his fundamentalist cultural crusade as a demographic threat to the white race in Europe and the United States from third world immigrants.

A staunch Roman Catholic and a conservative syndicated commentator, Buchanan, ran unsuccessfully for the Republican nomination for president in 1992 and 1996 and was the Reform Party's presidential candidate in 2000, where he failed miserably. In *The Death of the West*, Buchanan asserts that the West is facing four "clear and present dangers". Aside from a rapidly aging population, declining birth rates in Europe and the US, coupled with a population explosion in Africa, Asia and Latin America, the West now faces an apocalyptic threat.

"Not since the Black Death in the fourteenth century," he writes, *"has there been a greater threat to Western civilization."* He predicts that by 2050 only 10 per cent of the world population will be white. He adds: "Historians may one day call 'the pill' the suicide tablet of the West." Secondly, he contends that the "melting pot" no longer works in the US since we harbor millions of Mexican immigrants who constitute a *"nation within a nation"*. Similarly, Europe is being inundated by an *"Islamic-Arab-African invasion"*. These demographic changes in Europe and America are set to cause cataclysmic shifts in world power and result in balkanization of the United States.

Thirdly, the Bolshevik Revolution of 1917 ended with the fall of the Berlin wall but the counter-culture revolution started in the college campuses of America in the sixties has succeeded in de-Christianizing America, *"dethroning our God, vandalizing our temples and capturing our young"*. In a section called "Return of the Prophet", he states that *"now the signs are everywhere that Islam is rising again....In Europe, Christian congregations are dying, churches are emptying out and the mosques are filling up."*

Fourth, the ruling elite in the West have given up on nationalism and instead embraced the idea of globalization and world government. He quotes Strobe Talbott (former President Clinton's roommate at Oxford) who said: *"The term citizens of the world will assume real meaning in the 21st century."*

> *The hidden premise of this book, never explicitly stated, is that none of the non-European people migrating to America or Europe are competent to maintain the ways of life that make America and Europe the First World. But no where is this point argued openly.*

It is true that the West is facing a breakdown of the nuclear family and witnessing a decline in birth rates but to compare it to Black Death is balderdash. The 1968 book *The Population Bomb* by Paul Ehrlich made similar gloom and doom prophesies where exploding populations were going to exhaust the earth's resources well before the end of the twentieth century. If you read that book today it is outrageous in its unintended hilarity. In short, it is simply very difficult to predict the future.

Besides, even if Buchanan's whistling-in-the-wind prediction was true, so what? There are millions of other equally good human beings to fill up this imagined shortage of the white people in this world. But wait. There's the rub. Are those third world people of brown and black skin color not good enough to replace the master white race?

The hidden premise of this book, never explicitly stated, is that none of the non-European people migrating to America or Europe are competent to maintain the ways of life that make America and Europe the First World. But no where is this point argued openly.

Regarding the question of immigration and balkanization, Buchanan's book displays a gross ignorance of the complex process of acculturation and assimilation in American society. His book actually brings to mind the Nativist American crusades of the 1850s and 1920s when Buchanan's own Irish Catholic ancestors were called "white niggers" and told to go home.

To talk of balkanization of America because of diversity belies historic and contemporary reality. Repeatedly this myth of "nation within a nation" was successfully challenged by the Boston Irish, the New York Jews, the Chicago Italians and the Atlanta African-Americans. Add to that the recent immigrants, namely the Catholic Mexican-American or the Muslim Pakistani-American. They too are turning out to be the usual Americans in a multicultural society. Not only is the metaphor of the "melting pot" erroneous, but Israel Zangwill (whom Buchanan quotes with great flourish) who invented that famous term in 1908, in his later years returned to be a virulent Zionist.

The fact of the matter is that the USA has never been a monolithic, homogenized society. The false Eurocentric version of American history has already been discarded by eminent social historians like Nathan Galzer and Werner Sollers. Americans are now writing a more inclusive and accurate history of all the peoples who migrated to this continent starting with the Native Americans between about 14,000 and 35,000 years ago.

This objective American history clearly shows that America has always been a pluralistic society, receiving wave after wave of immigrants with different racial, cultural, ethnic and religious backgrounds from different parts of the globe. These diverse people did not melt into one supposed bland conformity nor indeed did this country break apart in some phantom balkanization. As Nathan Glazer has rightly pointed out, it is not accurate to call America a 'nation of nations'. Rather one pluralistic nation was created here made up of many races, cultures and religions.

> *The fact of the matter is that the USA has never been a monolithic, homogenized society. The false Eurocentric version of American history has already been discarded by eminent social historians. As Nathan Glazer has rightly pointed out, it is not accurate to call America a 'nation of nations'. Rather one pluralistic nation was created here made up of many races, cultures and religions.*

Turning to Buchanan's other "present dangers", his tirade against the liberal counter-culture is a contradiction in terms. According to him, if current trends in immigration and reproduction continue, white America will no longer be the First World. Yet it is the same white Americans of European descent who have debased America *"with out-of-wedlock children, homosexuality and militant paganism!"* Similarly, there is an incoherently argued case against globalization in favor of nationalism and a closed door policy.

In short, Buchanan's adamant book has no middle ground. He has failed to construct a sensible convincing case on the demise of the West. Frankly, this is the work of an alarmist politician who sees the world only in Manichean terms. (February 2002).

The death of the West By Patrick J. Buchanan

St Martin's   ISBN 0312285485   320pp.

Some Reviews of Authors' Books

"Writing Across Boundaries" Review 1

THE NATION, FEB 1, 2001.
WRITING ACROSS BOUNDARIES: by Javed Amir
Publisher: Sang-e-Meel Publications, Lahore
(Pakistan),
Reviewed by: *Professor Emeritus, Gilani Kamran.*

During the last two decades many Pakistani writers, poets and artists have visited Western countries, and written travelogues, yet their main interest has revolved around the intimate conduct of the American way of life. In Urdu, these safarnamas have quite a success, and were best sellers, but quite frankly these writing only gave surface information about the United States, and its multicultural society. Lately, however the problems of Pakistani families in the United States have appeared as the major theme of Urdu fiction.

These short stories have focussed on the difficulties of maladjustment in the host country. The cultural contradictions appear to cause uneasiness in feminist novel and short stories. But no writer has touched the essential state of American culture and has seen it in a transcultural and global perspective. Javed Amir has treated this much neglected aspect in his latest collection of writings titled Writing Across Boundaries.

It is an interesting work of intellectual realism, a pleasant cross section of learned opinion in American society. It makes smooth reading and opens up a scenario, which is not normally available to readers in any other medium. It is non-existent in Urdu writings.

This fascinating book has been published in Lahore; its writings draw their view-line from the West, and look upon an extended human scenario which is at present confronted with many challenges. Javed Amir is a retired diplomat and an old Ravian, and a keen observer of cultural undercurrents. He is perhaps the first Pakistani intellectual and writer who has formulated the question about the dilemma of becoming an American. His insight is enlightening, sympathetic and full of appeal. Unlike other Pakistani intellectuals, working in the universities in the United States, Javed Amir has rationalized the situation of a Pakistani immigrant against the amorphous state of cultural adjustment in the host country.

> *Javed Amir is a retired diplomat and an old Ravian, and a keen observer of cultural undercurrents. He is perhaps the first Pakistani intellectual and writer who has formulated the question about the dilemma of becoming an American.*

As an immigrant in multicultural society, Javed Amir has raised the primary question about his identity: Who I am? He states that an unbalanced and unresolved outsider-insider equation underlies the sensibility of an immigrant. There is centrifugal pull, which operates between the immigrant's original culture and the culture of the host country. In the common jargon, the immigrant has been variably described as an exile, an alienated human being, a person who is historyless, rootless and homeless.

As a person out of his own country, the immigrant has carried the burden of a nomadic existence which fails to provide him a spiritual shelter in a culture which has raised its foundations on material values. His race, color, language, religion and even his personal name make him an outsider, and deep in his psyche, his true self as an insider from a distant land, remains concealed to the view of the white population that makes the panorama of his environment.

All this may be an acute predicament for a less sophisticated individual, but in Javed Amir's case, it provides him with a double vision. His concern with writing, he points out, has saved him from identity crisis. Thus he has seen the outside world from the different cultural perspectives, and has redefined his movement from city to city, and from country to country as a free person, who has rediscovered his freedom in the shifting scenes of Western life.

All this gives him a strange sense of joy. He ceases to be an exile, a person without a country, a hermit, a refugee. He succeeds in placing himself in an emerging universal nation. This awareness, Javed Amir writes, has been provided to him by being an immigrant—a member of the America of the immigrants—which is growing in size, demographically, and multiculturally. As an immigrant, the man in his situation eventually becomes a past of America's future.

Nevertheless, in another essay on American cultural identity, his view has turned critical, and he has discussed the concept in the developing American intellectual opinion. He says that the word ethnicity has by now lost its sting of the other who is inferior, and a part of the brain dead Third World. The non-white population, it is suggested, has become 1/3rd by 2000 and by 2030, it is calculated to outnumber the white European population in the United States.

This demographic phenomenon has gradually made the other, the Ethnic, an equal member of the society and democratically it has made its presence felt meaningfully in the politics of the host country.

His essay titled Western intolerance of Islam is critical and enlightening, and it has placed the present state of Western attitude toward Islam in a right-size perspective. Javed Amir has quite clearly stated that hatred of Islam in the West, and the allegations about its apparent form in some circles of the American life are a legacy from the Milddle ages. The West, he writes, has never outgrown its medieval schizophrenic conception of Islam. He has reminded that in 1730, a French intellectual had portrayed the founder of Islam as a forerunner of the Age of Reason. He has also quoted Japanese Islamologist Murata who has defined Islamic values as "gentleness, love, compassion and beauty." Javed Amir writes: 'Modernism and liberalism are nothing new in Islamic culture. The liberal thrust of brilliant civilization in Muslim Spain was a result of the teachings of Muslims sages like Avicenna and Averroes."

Whatever be the nature of other problems in the life of an immigrant in the United States, Javed Amir's experience has proved that the immigrant rediscovers his essential being in that situation. He succeeds in watching his own soul in the mirror of a multicultural environment. This experience has also enabled him to look upon the scenario of human society in a constructive and positive manner, which has been an added attraction of his living in a country, which is shaping its future in multicultural dimensions. (Feb. 1, 2001).

Author's Note: Professor Emeritus Gilani Kamran was so gracious that without my knowledge he entered my book into the contest of the **Pakistan Prime Minister's Literary Awards for 2000** *under the auspices of the* **Pakistan Academy of Letters, Islamabad** *of which he was a senior member. My book won the First Prize for year 2000, but later the award was withdrawn on the ground that I was no longer a Pakistani citizen. I did, however, receive an email from The Academy congratulating me for the book. I came to know about all this after Prof. Kamran published the above article.*

"Writing Across Boundaries" Review 2

College Park Gazette (Published by *The Washington Post*).
December 3, 1998.
TWO LANDSCAPES IN ONE LIFE.
Beltsville author combines essays on adjusting to life in different cultures
By Karl Hille

Beltsville author Javed Amir has come to know two nations as home and be comfortable in both, an accomplishment some consider impossible.

"An Israeli writer once said, you cannot learn two landscapes in one life" said Amir, 53. "I disagree...I have come to make this as much a home as my home in Lahore (Pakistan)... in fact, Lahore has become a home away from home."

Amir's insight is enlightening, sympathetic and full of appeal. Unlike other Pakistani intellectuals, working in the universities in the United States, he has rationalized the situation of a Pakistani immigrant against the amorphous state of cultural adjustment in the host country.

Amir, a retired diplomat, published his second book this September, *Writing Across Boundaries,* a collection of essays about integrating into different cultures.

The 14 essays cover topics ranging from the nature of multiculturalism in America, the "changing soul" of American identity, the free capitalist market, the effects of television on literature, questions about belonging and exile, and a comic rendition of daily life in an American suburb. Through it all, Amir said, the book is united by the theme of "how an immigrant writer from another environment comes to terms with living in America."

A mirror of his own experiences, the essays have also helped Amir to understand his own multiculturalism, which he writes about in his book.

"I now see a continuity in my life from the East to the West. Lahore's river Ravi flows into the Washington's Potomac," Amir recited from his book.

Though he has traveled extensively with the Pakistan Foreign Service, Amir chose to settle in America and raise a family. He has lived in Beltsville for twenty years and calls it "a blessed place—different races, different people, co-existing peacefully together."

"This thing was always kind of teasing my mind," said Amir about his motivation to write the book. "What am I doing here? Who am I? Am I a Pakistani , or am I an American?"

Amir credits experience, literature and his children as major contributors to his successful integration into American culture.

He learned to adapt to other civilizations through his work as a diplomat. "As soon as you go out to another country, you realize that the things you thought were universal in your culture are not so in other parts of the world."

The largest contributor to his integration, however, has been his children.

> *A mirror of his own experiences, the essays have also helped Amir to understand his own multiculturalism, which he writes about in his book.*
>
> *"I now see a continuity in my life from the East to the West. Lahore's river Ravi flows into the Washington's Potomac."*

"My children nationalized me...I never knew the game of baseball, for example. In Pakistan we played cricket, from which baseball is derived..so when I sat with my children in Camden Yards in Baltimore I not only learned the game with my children but started to call America my home."

In Lahore, Amir had his poems published by age 14 in *The Pakistan Times*. He graduated with a Masters degree in English Literature securing first position in the Punjab University. After teaching at his alma mater and editing a monthly magazine *The Pakistan Review* for 5 years, in 1969 he got selected to The Pakistan Foreign Service at the top of his class.

Along the way he married Clemencia, a beautiful young lady from Colombia, whom he met in Brussels where both were studying French at the University. Incidentally, Amir speaks 5 languages: English, French, Spanish, Urdu and Punjabi.

In 1978, after his tours in Western Europe, Africa and Pakistan, Amir resigned from Pakistan Foreign Service and moved to Maryland where he is living the American Dream. Amir has 3 wonderful children and is now busy writing the second draft of his first novel.

"Writing Across Boundaries" Review 3

The Prince George's Journal
October 15, 1998.
Author Makes Mark *Writing Across Boundaries*
By DAVID PRESTON

One county resident is telling his tale of adaptation and interpretation to the world.

Javed Amir of College Park has written a book of essays titled *Writing Across Boundaries*.

Amir said the book was inspired by his need to articulate his "transition" from the East to the West.

Amir has lived, worked and written in five continents.

"The goal of the book is to further multicultural co-existence by brining the American people of diverse backgrounds together in art, religion and culture by emphasizing common grounds and by exposing false boundaries," Amir said.

Amir contends that race is not just skin color but rather a "construct of complex combinations of languages, history, class and culture."

"The Washington DC area is on the cutting edge of America's future and a wonderful place to be living in today," he added.

Amir did his Masters in English in Lahore, Pakistan and edited a monthly magazine, *The Pakistan Review*. He taught at the Government College, Lahore before being selected to The Pakistan Foreign Service. During his ten year career he served in Europe, Africa and Pakistan. Amir speaks 5 languages, thanks to his diplomatic career.

In 1978, he resigned from the diplomatic service and came to live in the DC area. His daughter, Sonia Amir is currently Miss Prince George's County and later on was elected Miss Maryland.

"Over the past 20 years in Maryland, my children have nationalized me. But, at the same time, I have internationalized them."

The book is available at several area book stores and at Amazon.com.

One county resident is telling his tale of adaptation and interpretation to the world.

Javed Amir of College Park has written a book of essays titled **Writing Across Boundaries.** *The book, says the author, was inspired by his need to articulate his "transition" from the East to the West.*

Resident Javed Amir on "Writing Across Boundaries"

by Ruth Garcia

During his diplomatic career as a foreign service officer for Pakistan, Javed Amir was assigned to several countries in five continents. In 1978 he resigned from the foreign service. He then migrated to United States and came to live in Beltsville. Over the past 20 years in Beltsville he and his wife, a Colombian, have raised three children. All of them are part of the St. Joseph School community where his wife works and his children attended school. His daughter Sonia Amir is the current "Miss Prince George's County 1998."

Javed Amir is fluent in five languages and has traveled, lived, and written worldwide. Currently, he is the editor of "The Pakistan Review", a monthly magazine published in Lahore, Pakistan. He divides his time in Beltsville, Europe, and Pakistan. The mix of Javed Amir multicultural personal and professional experiences came

In 14 essays, the book covers geographical, cultural, and linguistics boundaries such as ethnicity, religion, multicultural themes, art reviews, and a literary criticism among others. Javed Amir calls these "our spheres of mutual ignorance" because mankind tends to erect them to develop a divisive American society. "Writing Across Boundaries" presents with humor and ironic insights our common grounds in art, religion and culture to further multicultural co-existence among the American people and immigrants of different backgrounds.

"Writing Across Boundaries" points the reader in the right direction to better understand these spheres of mutual ignorance. The book is in hard cover with an attractive 4-color cover design of the Hindukush mountains, and 12 inside eye-catching illustrations. The book is available in area bookstores as well from Milestone Publications at (301)595-5372.

Beltsville author Javid Amir with his recent book "Writing Across Boundaries"

Beltsville News, October 1998.
Author Javed Amir with his recent book
"Writing Across Boundaries."

"Modern Soap" Review 1

DAWN, January 5, 2003

ARTICLE **5**

Best of Pakistani English literature of 2002

talent: few translations

By Muneeza Shamsie

...ries and skillful poems. The quality of work by some of the new writers is disappointing, but Pakistan offers so few opportunities for writers of English language fiction and poetry, that the journal has at least provided them with a platform and a voice,

...ries from *Turquoise* as well as other equally fine work from his previous collections, plus a new autobiographical sequence "This day's work: the story of my stories".

...three characters, a masseur, a prostitute and a eunuch who meet regularly near a shrine. The novel by the surprisingly young, 21 year old author, has been much

...Athar Tahir, as well as Badar Bakht and Leslie Levigne. The many admirers of the *Annual of Urdu Studies*, edited by M.U. Memon at the University of Wisconsin

...and literary texts used in the teaching of each national and provincial language over the centuries.

Meanwhile OUP is bringing out a series of books, *The subcontinent divided: a new beginning*, edited by Ian Talbot which will explore the

WRITERS WHO WERE IN PRINT IN 2002: (From top left clockwise) Javed Amir, Aamer Hussein, Hanif Kureishi, Hima Raza, Moniza Alvi, Muhammad Umar Memon, Tariq Rahman, Kamila Shamsie, Munir Niazi, Omar Kureishi, Asif Farrukhi, Jahan Ara Shahnawaz

...although it is a great pity that greater care was not taken over the proofreading.

The prolific Hanif Kureishi is now regarded as one of the best short story writers today. His new collection *The body* (Faber) has been described by *The Observer* as "a bleak, dark and impressive collection of stories". The title story, a novella, follows the misadventures of a sixty-year-old man, who has an operation which gives him a new young body and he seeks out new experiences under an assumed name.

The short fiction of the bilingual, Karachi-born expatriate Aamer Hussein traverses a myriad of cultures and literatures and is a celebration of storytelling across geographical boundaries. His third collection

...praised by C.Z. Abbas in *Dawn* "as a wonderful, unforgettable book" which touches upon "the deepest tragedy of human lives".

Somehow Musharraf Farooqi's first novel *Salar Jang's passion* (Summersdale) published in 2002 in Britain and a year earlier in India as *Passion in the time of termites* (HarperCollins), seems to have eluded Pakistani reviewers. In this satirical magic-realist tale the rich, septuagenarian Salar Jang searches for a bride and is obsessed with a film star, Madame Firdousi, while hordes of indestructible termites munch their way through the fictitious town of Purana Shehr playing havoc with all. There is some truly strong, vivid writing

Kamila Shamsie's third novel *Kartography* (Bloomsbury UK, OUP, Pakistan) is set amid Karachi's ethnic violence of the 1990's with flashbacks to the conflict of 1971. Translated into six languages the novel was selected by Tariq Ali in *The Independent*'s "2002 Books of the Year". He wrote: "Family secrets expose the historical amnesia that afflicts the country. It's a funny and affecting novel and a hopeful sign that a new generation of Pakistani writers are prepared to challenge sexual and political taboos." *Kartography* was also on *The Independent*'s second list "Books of the Year 2002" chosen by literary critics. There Jo Shapcott said " *Kartography* is still six

...Madison, will be glad to learn that the journal is now on a website www.urdustudies.com. This year's AUS has a special section in memory of Agha Shahid Ali, the talented Kashmiri American poet and translator, who died last year. The journal includes Laurel Steele's translations of Mustafa Zaidi's verses and extracts from Sajjad Zaheer's *Landan ki ek raat* translated by Ralph Russell. The many articles of interest range from "Female voices: women writers in Hyderabad at the beginning of the twentieth century" by Margrit Pernas, "Islamic and Islamicizing discourses" by Kelley Pemberton to "Government policies and the politics of the teaching of Urdu in

...human dimension of Partition. The series includes OUP's reprint of *Father and daughter: a political autobiography* by Jahan Ara Shahnawaz, which provides invaluable glimpses into the social and political developments from the late nineteenth century to Pakistan's first martial law, through the eyes of an extraordinary, dynamic and pioneering woman who saw events first hand as the daughter of Sir Muhammed Shafi, and in her own right, as an important political figure. The book, however, is rather dry reading for the general reader, for it lacks the life and colour necessary to a good autobiography; nor does it have the analytical content of a political book.

Javed Amir's novel "Modern Soap" is a light, enjoyable and entertaining satire about a bureaucrat who helps his relatives set up a soap factory in modern Pakistan. At the heart of the novel are tales of avarice, corruption and seduction in the corridors of power.

Muneeza Shamsie (Dawn: Best of Pakistani Novels in 2002)

"Modern Soap" Review 2

Modern Soap is a tale of two struggles: first, of three brothers wanting to ride the tide of change in a society entering the age of industry and urbanization and of fast life and corruption, with the break-up of traditional values of familial consideration and old notions of up-right patterns of life; second of a young son who, unawares, is sucked into a household with glittering exterior but a stifling inner soul that nursed an ancient tradition of fabled courtesans and artful manipulation of love. There are no heroes and no villains; it is a human story of a time of change and the stress and angst it inflicted on men.

In style, Javed avoids distorted mirrors, no phantasmagoria of Garcia Marquez that so overwhelmed the writings of the day and was followed in Pakistan by Basit Haqqani, a talented and imaginative author, for his allegorical novel "Pappio." Javed's canvass is realistic, his narrative simple but elegant, the pace is moderate and in that he captures the broad sweep of societal evolution and the minutia of individual tribulations. He watches the society breaking out of centuries of a crusted shell, but there are no butterflies, nor demons. It is the familiar landscape of human frailties and foibles, crass temptations of money, greed, opportunism and envy rolled together with nostalgia and qualms of conscience. On this canvass are occasional reflections of traditionally instilled morality that had a touch of innocence and of fading memory of tender mercies of the bygone days. He discerns no great purpose as he witnesses the roiling mix of old and new and conflict that grip the minds and spirit of men caught in the currents. Bringing out emotion in this stylistically realistic portrayal betrays that much of what Javed has written is autobiographical.

> *In Javed Amir's novel, there are no heroes and no villains; it is a human story of a time of change and the stress and angst it inflicted on men. It is the familiar landscape of human frailties and foibles, crass temptations of money, greed, opportunism and envy rolled together with nostalgia and qualms of conscience.*

The story begins with the three brothers who hailed from a rural depressed background but having climbed the social ladder in the urban setting of the new country, Pakistan, where opportunity for bureaucrats, professionals and businesses were unevenly opening up. High bureaucracy, drawing upon the meritorious tradition set by Imperial Britain, was the undisputed elite, and the middle brother had entered that hallowed sanctum of state power and authority. The youngest of the three had met with success in the nascent but fast emerging business community which, even though bereft of the status of the bureaucrat, was replete with accumulating capital. The eldest, Bhai, had become a respected lawyer, but was drawn towards an industrial venture "Modern Soap" with the middle brother as an invisible partner who was key to obtaining critical government approvals. When the youngest brother learns about the scheme, he is taken over by envy and feels cheated by the middle brother for his preference for Bhai over him as he considered himself to be naturally suited as a partner for the venture. He hits upon his own stratagem to discredit the middle brother though an intermediary who exploits the weakness of the middle brother's wife, a spirited lady morphed into a veritable wheeler dealer to make money using the position of her husband.

Amir avoids distorted mirrors, there are no demons nor butterflies. His canvass is realistic, his narrative simple but elegant, the pace is moderate and in that he captures the broad sweep of societal evolution and the minutia of individual tribulations.

The story develops against the backdrop of Ayub Khan's Pakistan of emerging industries, licenses, permits and the rise of the *nouveau riche*. The psychological havoc that the change wrought on to the traditional rural society is expressed through the experience of a simpleton village character Habil who Bhai inveigled into the Modern Soap venture. He is the unintended tragic figure who without comprehending why, is uneasy with his new circumstance. And when the venture collapses, he returns as a stranger to his rural setting he had left years ago. Meanwhile his family has fallen apart.

In parallel, Javed picks up on an exotic life story beginning several generations apart when a blue-eyed vixen, Billo, from the land of Cain (Afghanistan) enters the harem of Maharaja of Kashmir who like most of his ilk was a notorious debauch and an oppressive ruler under the tutelage of the colonial masters. She is forced to flee for her life back to her native land on discovering that she was pregnant with Maharaja's child - a death sentence for a concubine in the princely state. But she returns years later with her enchanting daughter, Paro, who seduces the aging Maharaja to part with many of the stately jewels including the famed crown jewel, the Regent, that had once so captivated, Billo, her mother. Three generations later, the Paro family still holds on to the gleaming stones as the stars of its fortune and the very essence of the myth and glamour of its lineage. Now in Pakistan, the family is planning to move to London; this is when its path crosses that of Shahid, the scion of the Bhai family.

Following the footsteps of his illustrious uncle, Shahid has joined the elite civil service and is set to proceed on an overseas assignment with diplomatic status. The tradition bound parents are keen to arrange a match befitting their son's newly acquired status. They are struck by the high-society profile of the Paro family while Shahid is smitten by the beguiling beauty and deceptive vulnerability of the intended betrothed, Beenu. He insisted on the marriage even when Bhai

> *It is my view that Amir has created a contemporary masterpiece in* **Modern Soap.** *In the first few chapters, Amir has tried to blend the mythic and the mundane in a masterly way. I would like to congratulate the author on the authenticity of the narrative.*

started having second thoughts and inkling about the dubious past of the Paro family. In time, Shahid moves to Paris and the Paro family to London along with the jewels shifted concealed under the privilege of diplomatic immunity. This mission accomplished, the dark side of the Paro family begins closing on the son in law, Shahid. Inheritor of an age-old courtesan tradition, the matriarch spun a web of pretension and play on emotions to bind the household with girls often dreaming of glamour, show biz and film acting and plaint male members whirling around to provide a protective cover. To belong, Shahid must yield. His wife, Beenu, stayed in London and insisted that Shahid abandon his job in Paris and start business that the family promised to set up for him in London. Confused, Shahid kept shuttling for weekend visits to the grand Paro family mansion in London that both lured him and suffocated him. The experience portrayed in the chapter "Living Dead" has a surreal touch.

Much against his instincts, Shahid is on the verge of taking the plunge and Beenu arrives to bring matters to a head. Fortuitously, Shahid's uncle, now retired, happens to be in Paris. Already his elder brother, Bhai had entreated him to do something to rescue his son. The uncle meets Shahid and Beenu at their apartment for a courtesy visit and makes a brilliant proposal that as it unfolds exposed the hollowness and perfidy of the Paro family business proposition importantly to Beenu. She agonizes over the revelation, but the family bonds prove to be overpowering, and she leaves. The uncle's stratagem works to shake Shahid out of a spell.

How should we look at the novel? Perhaps, Javed is just trying to tell a beautiful story partly based on his personal experience that he thought must be told, or does he intend it to more than that. He appears to leave that question to the reader to answer. The story, however, has a happy ending. Broken and forlorn in Paris, our protagonist, Shahid is restored by the love and care of an exceptional person who hailed from a world apart. He finds his Paradiso in a simple, honest but universal culture that breathes like fresh air. Incidentally, Javed's other significant literary contribution is titled "Writing Across Boundaries."

Review of *Modern Soap* by Riaz Mohammad Khan.

"Modern Soap" Review 3

One of the things that struck me most about *Modern Soap* was the theme running through 'The Prologue,' Land of Cain I, Land of Cain II, and Land of Cain III. In a few pages, Amir has tried to blend the mythic and the mundane in a masterly way. Out of these chapters emerge powerful themes—of love and hate, possession and dispossession, of pride and degradation, of forces that are easily discernible and unknown.

> *The headings of the different chapters come to symbolize the scenes they convey. GOR for example conveys the sights and smells of bureaucratic life, which has unmistakable reality. Both Harappa and Gujrat represent different shades of meaning, which is so well reflected through the underlying nuances of prose.*

The other feature that I thoroughly savored was the artistic dexterity with which Amir has captured the flavor of society and times that we all have been witnesses and participants of. The headings of the different chapters come to symbolize the scenes they convey. GOR for example conveys the sights and smells of bureaucratic life, which has unmistakable reality. Both Harappa and Gujrat represent different shades of meaning, which is so well reflected through the underlying nuances of prose.

Then there is the web of events entangling the lives of individuals and families, which constitutes the narrative of the novel. The journey, the big scheme, Akmal's party, the arranged marriage, the forgery, the bribe, the revenge and loot are not only inter-connected events, but in a sense, the very stuff of life that we have known at first hand. I would like to congratulate the author on the authenticity of the narrative.

The most important aspect of course, is what lies at the heart of the novel—the probing into of human relationships—parent-son, brother-brother, husband-wife, rural and urban cousins, and families with such similar and dissimilar backgrounds. The strains in the chain of human relationship throw up configurations, which reflect psychological, cultural and social realities, which makes us see beyond what meets the eye.

It is my view that Amir has created a contemporary masterpiece in *Modern Soap*. I read it cover to cover with undiluted interest—such was the power of events and characters portrayed and the telling portrait of the times that we have lived in and I still live in.

Review by Ejaz Rahim.

"Modern Soap" Review 4

Poisoned Relations
by **Abdul Basit Haqqani**

Modern soap is about greed and the corruption it leads to. More insidiously, greed poisons human relations, even the closest and most sacred.

Javed Amir tells the story of three brothers of modest, lower middle-class origins. Maq, is a senior civil servant who has the contacts, and in his official capacity, himself wields the power, to enable entrepreneurs to make millions. His elder brother, Bhai, is a lawyer though not a very successful one. He is dependent on some of the favors he receives from the third brother, Akmal, who is already an established industrialist.

From the very beginning, however, we are aware of the fact that greed is at work poisoning the relations between brothers. Akmal bears a grudge against Maq, because the latter has not helped him to obtain the licenses and permits without which the wheels of capital have never run in Pakistan. Maq's abhorrence of nepotism, which was openly and shamelessly indulged in by Pakistan's first military ruler, is resented not only by his brother but also by his wife. Being forced to act against his better instincts for the sons of the President and the political cronies of the dictator, it is only a question of time before Maq succumbs to the temptations that his position puts in his way.

> *In the novel, Americanisms abound. Thus, "Momentarily, Habil came down" (momentarily being American for "in a short while") or he "could not help obsessing". This is not meant as criticism because English is a foreign language but such usage is faintly disturbing to Pakistani readers because we are brought up on the Queen's English.*

When he does decide to start a "benaami" factory to produce modern soap, which is described as a great contribution to industrial development, he turns to Bhai, the eldest brother, rather than to Akmal who is the only one experienced in business. These two are already beyond rapprochement. With Bhai not immune from suspicion, they turn to a cousin, Habil, from their village who is made the nominal owner of the factory. Being a rustic innocent, Habil is not expected to betray the trust reposed in him. He emerges as one of the few decent characters in the book, though being a former patwari, it stretches one's credulity to believe in his pristine innocence.

Shahid, Bhai's son and a brilliant boy is selected for the Foreign Service. He is married to a predatory girl, the daughter and granddaughter of concubines who dazzle Shahid's simple parents with their wealth and social connections. The girl's family uses Shahid for devious ends. Once married, their daughter would obtain a diplomatic passport and be able to smuggle out the family's wealth in precious stones, including the Regent, a fabulous diamond that the grandmother had stolen from the Maharaja of Kashmir.

As the soap factory is being built, suspicions begin to poison relations between Bhai and Maq, while Akmal, the third brother, sets spies on them, including Fasaadi, who seems to like nothing better than creating a rift between the brothers. Mutual suspicion leads to a total breakdown and legal maneuvers by Maq and his wife to take complete control of Modern Soap and to oust Bhai.

By now the Field Marshal's regime is tottering. The second military dictator of the country busies himself projecting the image of a clean administrator, dismissing 303 civil servants. Maq, who has gone on from setting up a factory to the even baser crime of accepting bribes and commissions, is one of them. While this is going on, young Shahid's marriage also breaks up and greed for wealth and social status both lead to disappointment.

Modern Soap is a realistic tale. Javed Amir is meticulous in providing the exact time and locale of the story. Thus, it begins in 1965 and ends some three years later. Most of the action takes place in Lahore of that time and some localities and buildings are specifically mentioned and described. Some of the events and personalities are historic. Scrupulous exactness about public facts makes the reader wonder whether the book is a roman a clef. Realism may help the reader imagine a scene or situation but has pitfalls for the author, particularly one who has not lived in the place for several years and now lives in America..

> *The important thing about Modern Soap is that it addresses an issue of great public importance, that is, corruption. In dealing with its human implications, the book reveals a private, familial dimension in a psychologically convincing manner.*

For example, no one would refer to any locality of Lahore as "downtown". Other Americanisms abound. Thus, "Momentarily, Habil came down" (momentarily being American for "in a short while") or he "could not help obsessing". This is not meant as criticism because English is a foreign language but such usage is faintly disturbing to Pakistani readers because we are brought up on the Queen's English. **

The important thing about *Modern Soap* is that it addresses an issue of great public importance, that is, corruption. In dealing with its human implications, the book reveals a private, familial dimension in a psychologically convincing manner. One wishes Amir had also touched on the public aspect to reveal how, given the economic framework of licensing and the social reality of personal, feudal relationships, nepotism and corruption are almost inevitable and the public malaise breeds the private disease. But it is the author's book and we must thankfully enjoy what he has offered us.
(*Dawn, July 2003*).

Modern Soap By Javed Amir, Alhamra Publishing, Saudi Pak Tower, Jinnah Avenue, Islamabad. ISBN 969-516-075-1, 204pp.

**Author's note: First of all, English is not a foreign language in Pakistan. It is a second language, as explained in the essay in this book titled, "Many Faces of Global English." Secondly, the reviewer seems to forget that although the novel is based in Pakistan, it was mainly distributed and read in the USA where no one was disturbed by its "Americanisms."

Smith & Campbell's Pharmacy and Ghulam Rasool Building, Lahore- Photo taken in 1922. *Smith & Campbell's Pharmacy premises are seen at the left-hand corner of the building. 'Ghulam Rasool Building' is on the right. Ghulam Rasool Building was completed in 1916. Famous Ferozsons Book Store is located in this building. It is adjacent to Al-Falah Building near Charing Cross on The Mall. Javed Amir worked in Ferozsons, 1965-69 as Associate Editor of The Pakistan Review.*

Government College, Lahore. *The author was a student (1960-66) where he did his M.A. securing First position in the University winning the Munshi Ghulab Singh Gold Medal and then worked as Lecturer in English (1967-1969). He joined The Pakistan Foreign Service in 1969.*

A Bit of Nostalgia

I have no name for that
Feeling is all. (Goethe)

In keeping with the general theme of this book, where thoughts are not supposed to die, I decided that it would be fitting to bestow upon some long forgotten memories the immortality of re-print. This is a brief glimpse of literary Lahore, the city where I grew up as a child in the 50's and a youth in the 60's. As I look back, it really is like Proust's *Temps Perdu*. Perhaps the ideal way to reminisce is to recall those unforgettable images, juvenile creativity and undying thoughts as they occurred either in spoken or in written form in those bygone days, forty to fifty years ago.

My Farewell Dinner Address-on behalf of the Class of 1969-- at the Civil Service Academy, Lahore July 1970:

Mr. Director, Honorable Guests, Ladies and Gentlemen,

In his farewell address to the High Court Bar Association the late Justice Kayani remarked that he was not sure whether he spoke with a heavy heart or a light one: sometimes it was heavy, he said, and. sometimes light. Tonight, no better words can express more vividly my own predicament. Poised as we are between the devil and the deep sea, the glorious period of probation over and the somewhat uncertain future ahead of us we feel as if we have just had our last supper. In retrospect as we look back at the slings and arrows that were inflicted on some of our more sensitive colleagues at the Civil Service Academy, one cannot, at times, help admire the reassuring though uncharitable theme of good riddance.

Ladies and Gentlemen, it all began, in the unearthly hours of a soft October morning when dressed in shorts we found ourselves involved in what was euphemistically called physical training or P.T. for short. Indeed it was here in these lawns that I discovered for the first time that the moment of my greatness flickered. Personally, I had nothing against early morning P.T. but for the instructor who kept on yelling at one of our more heavy-set probationer colleague, that it was difficult to figure out whether he was coming or going. In the words of the military instructor--who knew how to massacre the English language--our friend was a "fireball on two legs."

Next morning, we bookworms faced another pre-dawn harrowing experience. This was the horse riding lesson, meant I presume, in all sincerity to turn us into patriotic and daring civil servants. When Channan Khan our age-old coach blurted "trot" in his merciless voice and the horses took off, it left yours truly stony with unwavering misery. Soon I had a taste of more things to come. Not only did I have the exclusive distinction to fall off a standing horse but also the whole traumatic experience of riding these beasts was like a drowning man's instantaneous vision of life. Having had to wallow in distress, L&G, we developed a cult of neo-stoicism after the Greek philosophers with this amended line of Drayton as our cardinal principle:

Since there is no help, come, let us ride and depart!

L&G, forgive me for having destroyed this largely romantic line of Drayton. In this regard l am particularly conscious not to hurt the feelings of a large number of fledgling, sometimes shaken, freshly married husbands of our Academy. According to one such romantic hero and authority on these conjugal matters the best way to seduce is via Greek mythology: "Your face like Helen can launch a thousand ships" is not an unusual compliment for a face capable of sinking a million. In fact all my friends except one is convinced that there is nothing worse than being a bachelor. Now this dear friend is convinced that love is a condition of the mind when the mind is out of condition. Very ably he defines marriage as a lottery in which men stake their pockets and women their liberty and in the end both win a consolation prize. Instead of being posted to Denmark where he could declare "frailty thy name is woman," our young Hamlet, surprise, surprise, is headed for Paris.

L&G, I do not wish to take more of your time. Suffice to say that today our hearts are heavy not with the thought of parting from the Civil Service

Academy, for there is no parting in the intellectual world, but the thought of that which has happened during the year. Contrary to the popular misconception about this institution, which has been portrayed sometimes as an ivory tower, it is here that we ceased to live in dreamland. Today as we look around, we see a directionless drift in our nation, of little men unable to rise to the dark and demanding challenges that we all face in our country.

In Pakistan with most of us the problem today is that beneath a thin veneer of western attitudes, which we have accepted, life is still running in medieval grooves. Our generation in particular fails to read the minutes of the last meeting. Characteristically, we do not believe in reading anything at all. We disavow the dictum live and learn. L&G, ideally speaking though one would like to live and learn yet such is the jest of life that once you have lived it is either meaningless to learn or by the time you have learnt it is too late to live

Thank You.

The Mask

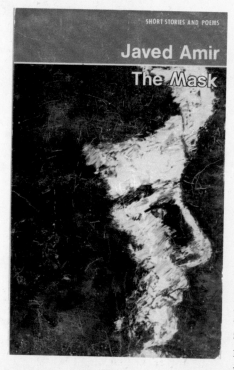

I HAVE not written for a long time now. After that night, I had made up my mind never to write again. But you know we are all apt to break pledges. And then, I have changed in this long, dreary period. Now I enjoy with holding the so-called moments of inspiration. I have ceased to feel. One thing, I am no longer disgusted. Yes, I am not fed up with life any more. Only, I have grown to be something different, different from all that has been. The absurd, romantic longing to inquire into the mystery of my heart, beating so wild, so deep within me, has faded into the quagmire of a new barren emotion almost cruel. Now I hate myself. Around me lingers the shadow of my mask. Perhaps, this is too inadequate an emotion for modern times? No, you don't think so. This hobble of being alive is not so serious after all ! What if you suffer and you are alone: *magna civitas, magna solitudo*.

My glance darted into the night. The headlights rotate on the brown, dusty gravel of the nightclub and illumine white poppies at the far end of the lawn. I feel the cold smoothness of the steering clenched within my grasp like the icy numbness of frozen flesh. The car whimpers and groans as it comes to a halt. I glue my eyes to a signboard. Behind, the newly trimmed lawn shines hauntingly! Why is everything appearing so strange to me ? Like old days when...No, I am no longer in love with life. I have grown impersonal. But why this feigned objectivity? This dread of exploring into the meaning of meaning? I know I am not extraordinary. I don't want to feel extraordinary in any way. Yet I have no peace, but...let me warn you not to be misled by my words. I am not what I am.

As I come out of the car, they all join me, and we enter the ball-room. Tonight, I don't want to feel like a stranger in their midst even if they appear to be the habitual diseased animals. I listen to their filthy, mundane gossip with remarkable ease. He was saying something about the new cabaret dancer in the club. Greedily, I look around and transfix her with my hungry gaze. There she sits with a certain air of non-accessibility with large beautiful eyes, draped with long silken lashes. I feel I must have her. Suddenly, I remember. Just after the rain. She too thought that she was inaccessible! ... *the night when we two were together, with the volleying rain and the tossing breeze. On the wet platform we walked a long way. But I was alone .all the time! You know what people say? The past is dead. I don't believe them - but lost memories will always haunt you......*

No ! No ! not again.

You cannot afford to be sentimental in this world. What you have to be is cruel. Life nowadays is jaded with a sick hurry and we are all victims of our divided selves. By now, you must have known that I abhor what I actually love and reject what I definitely believe. The faint tortuous memory of the night on the wet platform returns to my mind. I wish it would not return. But there it is! The roof of the iron sheets had leaked heavily. The passengers huddled into dry Corners. She did not know that I was there to receive her. Neither did he. I remember, then, when we two were together. Strangely enough, I felt as if I was alone. That she was not there. Non-existent. We walked a long way hand in hand. I was drenched with rain and so was she. But, he was there too! Almost dry. Not a drop on his body. Dry and cunning, but soaked with envy. He had, cheated me. So handsome and godly in appearance, he was incapable of evil. I was betrayed by that which is false within. When the rain stopped, I was lost and saw nothing around me but the shadow of the mask.

But why should I tell you all this? I do not know! Sometimes, when the noise of the rain feverishly beating within me becomes unbearable, I ask who am I? What is it that I live for? Why have I worn this guilty veneer of ugliness wrapped in lust and deceit? Yet, though I ask these futile questions, I know that there is no escape from the enemy within.

Yes, yes we are all self-destructive, there is no escape from one's self. The mask is within us all, the mysterious enemy ready to grab you and lure your soul into darkness.

Where is that justice that conveys our poisoned chalice to our own lips? No we do not have justice here! No peace! No love! No truth to pierce the mask of appearance! I know he has destroyed my conscience. I hate him for the harm he has done me, and yet I love him. It is a strange attachment.

I admire the unsensational brilliance of his petty trickeries, knowing full well that it is he who has inflicted this mask on me and transformed me into a dumb sufferer. Each evening, I imagine the volleying rain and the tossing breeze torture my soul. Yes! Yes! The past never dies. It returns. And lost memories always haunt you. I see the wound afresh. I have discovered its meaning, its pang: the poisoned chalice is always before me in the night. For the first time I am telling you the truth. You don't believe me? I can see that. I don't care for what you believe. After that night I have never been the same again.

But why have I to tell you all this? I should not come here every night. I must leave now. I hear them giggle. Yes, I must leave. But wait. What about this mask of ambiguity? Yes I need more ambiguity! I am no longer afraid of life! Tonight I don't want to feel like a stranger in their midst. I will listen to their filthy gossip with remarkable ease...

And then, I will have her.

"A Bit of Nostalgia" 1967-1969

The
Pakistan Review

DECEMBER, 1967

COVER STORY
"THREE YEARS
TV PLAYS
by
S. JAVED AMIR

S. JAVED AMIR

Javed Amir has been our Associate Editor for the last three years. At present, he is also teaching in the Govt. College, Lahore, from where he did his M. A. in 1966, Besides, 'The Review' he has been published in a number of journals in the country like 'Inspirations', 'The Orient Literary', 'Silhouette' etc. Occasionaly he writes for 'The Pakistan Times'.

THE ADDICT

(1)

HE woke up from his deep slumber.: It was evening. As the old chaudhri opened his eyes on his tattered, sinful bed he felt the growing terrors settling on his waking life. The vacant Haveli was staring horridly at him. He seemed to have lived for a hundred years in that one, evening nap.

"Shamsu! where are you?"'

The only servant was preparing 'hooka' for the old man.

"Here I am chaudhri jee."

"Where is Walayat, Shamsu?"'

"He has work to do. Already the Haveli needs repairs".

"What time is it, Shamsu?"

"The sun has set. I have lit the lamps at the main door."

"And what day is it, Shamsu 1"

"Don't you know chaudhri jee it is doomsday, I mean friday."

"But why haven't you brought my bowl of water?"

He was beginning to feel the diminishing hues of his grains of opium.

He must always be intoxicated to

overcome this horrible guilt. But, the servant growled:

"You must not take it again Chaudhri jee. It is bad for your health. And then your son-"

He knew it was not his fault for whenever he asked the time, the Haveli answered 'It is time for opium'.

"I wonder what has kept him so late in the hospital?"

He opened a packet full of Circean charms, cut into small round drops, into his wide mouth and pouring water after it, swallowed the black mass in one big gulp.

"Go and call him, Shamsu. It is getting too late."

He was feeling elated. But, of late he had grown weak. Now the charms and sunless abysses of his dreams were boring him. Drop by drop the charms of life were dying out. Life was oozing away. And then, this summer heat that blew into the village, had made existence unbearable. It was as if for centuries that he had lay on his deceitful bed facing this cruel, hot storm with its dusty whirlwinds as they swept into the courtyard and against the decaying Haveli. Now as Shamsu banged the main door after him a shadow of urgency crept into the place. He was feeling wearier than ever before.

He shouldn't have taken a larger dose, he felt. It would surely upset his stomach. And then his son, Walayat would have to resort to all kinds of nasty medicines and injections. And injections he detested. But then, he loved his son who was a doctor and who had left the city and come to live with him in the ancestoral Haveli only to look after his beloved father. All of a sudden he blurted:

"I wonder what is keeping him so late in the hospital. I don't like this frivolous habit of staying out-of-doors so late. And, he knows he has a sick father to attend to...."

He was his last passion in life. He was going to redeem the otherwise lecherous family. So the old man was always fussy about his prized possession. He knew that the gaping walls of the ominous ruins around him needed repair which his son would provide. And he felt regenerated and afraid at the same time. He was wondering why Walayat had refused Jameela's father that day? Was he interested in somebody else? The old man recovered himself and chuckled understandingly:

"He told me he will remain a bachelor all his life. Throughout his years he has tried to be different from his progenitors."

Chaudhri's own grand-father, the one time renowned Jagirdar had spent no less than a fortune on his son's marriage. He sold half his lands to get the money. They had to bring all that money on a cart---and in sacks full of silver coins---as well as hire a gunman. One day, the Chaudhri thought, he would arrange Walayat's wedding in the same grand manner.

"But why hasn't he come home till now?"

And he stopped dreaming.

(II)

The sun rose above his ugly bed. Now the dust was raging warmer. It was beginning to suffocate him. He turned the pillow sideways, clinging to the cooler part with his mouth wide open. The Ramadan of his abstinence was over. He felt the dust revealing millions of painful memories.

"Shamsu, what is the time?"

"Your son does not want to come to the Haveli"

"Bring me the bowl of water"

"I can't He is asleep in the hospital"

At this the old man clasped the blanket in pain. In the ominous silence, the old chaudhri felt as if the Hcrveli was grinning at him, with its sombre face.

"Shamsu, he promised his mother he wouldn't do it again" "But why did he sleep in the , hospital, Chaudhri, jee?"

If he had stayed in the city he could have earned a lot more and far quicker. He should have lived away from the Haveli, this callous, inhuman enemy of his forefathers.

He knew this. Then why did he chose to be a deliberate victim. He could have escaped heredity. He was different. He was not like him at all. Then why had he slept all night in the hospital? The patients would have turned 'him mad. And then... .He knew Walayat shouldn't have been born.' And throughout his years he thought he was going to different!

And yet he will be similar to that filth, that horrible infection in his blood.

"Yes, Shamsu, let him sleep. We must not repair the ruins of this heartless coquette. We shall have no more marriages. We must let these walls crumble to dust" .

Now the burden of life drifted away. He saw it all: He was the wound and the blade; he was the victim and the executioner! But he was feeling relieved. He had nothing to hope for. As usual in this Haveli, life had given birth to death. And he saw it all as clearly and vividly as an early morning dream.

"Shamsu, give me that bowl" he spoke loudly. Grabbing it from the servant he flung the clay utensil far into the courtyard. It hit into one of the parched walls, splashing some water on the dust, and landed on the floor. Uncanny as it seemed the bowl did not break.

"The Addict" was published in *The Pakistan Review*, January 1968.

Evening

I am alone in the room...
The house is brooding in darkness
For I have put out the lights.
The big iron gates of the garage
Strike vacantly against the cemented walls:
No one is home
They have all gone to the club.
The book on the table lies open;
A short while ago
I read some pages
Of dusty facts worn-out through the ages
Now I can read no more!
He looks at me
Dismayed, worried.
The ash of cigarettes is before me
Always this same futile ash
When I am alone in the room.
I notice there is a storm in the lawn
Dusty storm that sweeps into the courtyard;
I listen to what the wind says:
A howling tune that whispers in agony
And I rejoin in pain.
What music, what symphony
Can these dull chords of life attain?
He switches on the lamp
Suddenly the dust outside looks
Warm and beautiful!
'Why have you put out the lights?' he asks,
'Come out and sit in the lawn
It is so pleasant outside:
The iron gate bang against the cemented walls !
Why am I feeling so sad?
And I hear him add
'The bolt has been broken:'
Shut up! Leave me alone!
Well....
Why am I feeling so sad?

"A Bit of Nostalgia" 1963

THE PAKISTAN TIMES
Magazine

The Poet of the East.

21ST APRIL, 1963

SONNET

The Heavens were as calm as a lonely
heath
The waves of the sea rolled on,
as if to breathe
The sultry atmosphere
Presently the horizon was enveloped in
darkness
It spread on the yawning foam
of the ocean
The pleasant breeze shook the
silent atmosphere
It began to rain
Oh, Lord! Such blissful scenes
Are but an adoration of your greatness
The starry sky, the silent
night
The howling wind, the fearful
storm
How the world lives and
moves
Makes us believe that there is something
Greater than we know!

JAVED AMIR,
Lahore

I conclude this sentimental recollection of my juvenilia with these lines of
Dante Alighieri, I frequently recited in those days:

Fixing my gaze upon the Eternal Light
I saw enclosed within its depths
Bound up with love together in one volume
The scattered leaves of all the universe:
Substance and accident, and their relations
Together fused in such a way
That what I speak of is one simple flame.

Acknowledgements

Clemencia and Javed in Carmel-by-the-Sea, CA.
November 2012.

I am most grateful to Khaled Ahmed for his fascinating Foreword to my book. He is truly a world-class thinker and writer, and befittingly was awarded Pakistan's highest civilian honor, namely The Presidential Pride of Performance. From the days he edited *The Ravi* and the short stories that he contributed to *The Pakistan Review*, I have been an admirer of the depth of his knowledge and talent. Indeed I share with him a visceral antipathy for the hideous distortion of Islam by some in Pakistan. His courageous and scholarly analysis in his book "Sectarian Wars" is noteworthy. Needless to say, he is a master of thought, what the French call *maître* à *penser*. We are all proud of this Lahore treasure.

Readers of my book must have noticed that like any other art form, Essay writing is really about raising questions, not answering them. "Art is a form of gymnastics" wrote Umberto Eco, "in which we practice to understand what we don't understand."

Second, it was pointed out to me that it was rather premature on my part to talk of old age when I am still a middle-aged person. If you look at the cover of this book, the road (of my life) is at a bend and, therefore, the book is an attempt at imagining in advance what old age should be. It is a sort of a pre-empting exercise. Easier said than done, I confess.

Although many learned books and wise teachers prepared me over the years, as I look back, I can see how *Thought Never Dies* was born. It all began accidentally, of course, in 2008 as I drove alone on a dusty country road known as Route 28 from El Paso, Texas to Mesilla, New Mexico. That was the first time I ever ventured into New Mexico and instantly fell in love with this enchanting land and the spirituality it emanated. The very next year, with Cle as an incomparable companion, we drove to Santa Fe and on to Abiqui with its Ghost Ranch and the Padernal of Georgia O'Keeffe fame.

However, it was not until a year later when Riaz Mohammad Khan and I flew to Santa Fe and drove to Taos and back on the fabled High Road that my gestation period ended. Sitting in a Café on Canyon Road near the Santa Fe Plaza I knew something was afoot. While I was quoting John Muir, Riaz was challenging me with Mirza Ghalib and in that exchange my essay titled "The Sacred" was born. After that, it was off to the races and in quick succession, with serendipity as my guide, I managed to write a dozen essays within two years, resulting in this book.

As we know, writing a book is the easy part. To get it published in a suitable manner is another story. Once again my dear friend Riaz, who has been my guiding light for 40 years, came to the rescue. He introduced me to Bakhtiar uddin Ahmed of Imprint*publishing* who has been a joy to work with. He is truly a talented designer and publisher and I am thankful to him for his dedication and hard work.

I also have to thank my colleague, Ejaz Rahim, with whom I have shared a life-long love of literature starting in Government College, Lahore in the sixties. Ejaz has always encouraged me at every step in completing this book and read the manuscript with great interest, intelligence and warmth. It is in times like these that I remember how valuable old friends are and what a joy it is to have them. As Yeats once wrote:

Think where man's glory most begins and ends
And say my glory was I had such friends.

I am also grateful to Marie Arana, former Book Editor of *The Washington Post*, Carole Sargent, Director of Scholarly Publications, Georgetown University and David Cohen of "Politics and Prose" Bookstore for providing me with insightful comments, after I inflicted my manuscript on them. They are truly very gracious and generous people.

I will be remiss if I do not mention Gloria Silvestre Khokhar who along with Javed Khokhar are not only great friends but also an extremely helpful and loving couple. Gloria is an accomplished copy editor and she painstakingly read every word of the manuscript and did a highly professional job for which I will be forever thankful.

Finally, there is Clemencia, the love of my life, to whom this book is dedicated. Together we have traveled to at least thirty countries abroad and crisscrossed by road almost all the scenic drives and national parks in the Unites States and Canada. And we are not done yet! Besides, Cle's boundless optimism and irrepressible Latin humor has literally transformed my life. The other morning she asked: "Why were you up so early?" I replied with my usual grandiloquence: "I was writing my dear. Don't you know what Goethe said: 'Write at dawn, skim the cream of the day'." And you know what she replied? "But you cannot skim the cream, dear. Remember you are lactose intolerant."

To that I replied after a brief pause:

Grow old with me
The Best is yet to be!

You see I am hopeless.

November 14, 2013.   J.A.

Since some of the material in this book has been published previously, we gratefully acknowledge permission for reprinting them along with reproduction of illustrations, Editorial Cartoons etc. from the following to avoid copyright infringement:
Dawn Newspaper
The Washington Times
The Washington Post
New York Review of Books
World Press Review
Harper Perennials Publishing
Sunday News, New York
Prince George's Journal
Beltsville News
The Nation
New York Ganz Collection
Metropolitan Museum of Art, New York
Santa Fe Museum of Fine Arts
National Gallery of Art, Washington DC
Library of Congress
WETA
Le Soir, Bruxelles
Le Soliel, Dakar
El Espectador, Bogota.

Every effort was made to obtain necessary permission and we apologize if inadvertently any source was not acknowledged.

Imprint_publishing_